Keys to Unlocking Depression:

An Internationally Known Depression Expert Tells You What You Need to Know to Overcome Depression

by

Michael D. Yapko, PhD

Also by Michael D. Yapko, PhD

The Discriminating Therapist: Asking "How" Questions, Making Distinctions, and Finding Direction in Therapy. Yapko Publications, 2016.

Essentials of Hypnosis, 2nd edition. New York: Brunner/Mazel, 2015.

Trancework: An Introduction to the Practice of Clinical Hypnosis, 4th edition. New York: Routledge, 2012.

Mindfulness and Hypnosis: The Power of Suggestion to Transform Experience. New York: Norton, 2011.

Depression is Contagious: How the Most Common Mood Disorder is Spreading Around the World and How to Stop It. New York: The Free Press, 2009.

Hypnosis and Treating Depression: Applications in Clinical Practice (Editor). New York: Routledge, 2006.

Treating Depression with Hypnosis: Integrating Cognitive-Behavioral and Strategic Approaches. New York: Brunner/Routledge, 2001.

Hand-Me-Down Blues: How to Stop Depression from Spreading in Families. New York: St. Martin's, 1999.

Breaking the Patterns of Depression. New York: Random House/Doubleday, 1997.

Suggestions of Abuse: True and False Memories of Childhood Sexual Trauma. New York: Simon & Schuster, 1994.

Free Yourself from Depression. Emmaus, PA.: Rodale Press, 1992.

Hypnosis and the Treatment of Depressions: Strategies for Change. New York: Brunner/Mazel, 1992.

Brief Therapy Approaches to Treating Anxiety and Depression (Editor). New York: Brunner/Mazel, 1989.

When Living Hurts: Directives for Treating Depression. New York: Brunner/Mazel, 1988.

Hypnotic and Strategic Interventions: Principles and Practice (Editor). New York: Irvington, 1986.

Keys to Unlocking Depression:

An Internationally Known Depression Expert Tells You What You Need to Know to Overcome Depression

Yapko Publications
P.O. Box 487
Fallbrook, California, U.S.A. 92088-0487

For information about permission to reproduce selections from this book, write to Permissions, Yapko Publications, P.O. Box 487, Fallbrook, CA 92088-0487
or submit contact form found on www.yapko.com

For information about special bulk purchases, please contact Special Sales, Yapko Publications, P.O. Box 487, Fallbrook, CA 92088-0487
or submit contact form found on www.yapko.com

ISBN: 978-0-9910796-2-9 (pbk)
ISBN: 978-0-9910796-1-2 (ebk)

Dedication

To Mom and Dad with love and admiration

Acknowledgments

My wife, Diane, is the inspiration for this book and for almost everything else I do. We're going on our fortieth year of marriage, and there isn't a day that goes by that I'm not grateful for her being my everything. Her love, support, and dazzling smile still make me deeply aware of how very lucky I am.

My family and friends are, individually and collectively, amazing people. I'm so grateful for all you have added to the richness of my life.

My colleagues and workshop sponsors have inspired me to better clarify and organize my ideas for my presentations around the world. But my clients have been the source of my motivation and creativity for helping those who suffer from depression. My work is infinitely better and more meaningful because of them.
Thank you all from the bottom of my heart.

MDY

Disclaimer: This book addresses the mood disorder known as major depressive disorder, or major depression, in general terms. It is not a substitute for professional diagnosis and/or treatment by a qualified mental health professional for any individual. It provides readers with an expert's informed perspectives in order to help guide a sensible recovery from the burden of depression.

Table of Contents

Introduction

This book is intended to help provide a life raft of clarity to those who are treading water in the sea of confusion about depression. It offers a straightforward, plainly spoken perspective about depression and its treatment based on current science and the clinical judgment I can offer based on more than three decades of specializing in treating people suffering depression. Since depression is greatly influenced by your own perspective, developing a clear and effective perspective is a vitally important first step to a depression-free life. This book discusses some of the most important things you will need to know if you want to better understand and overcome depression.

Someone wise once said, "The best way to predict the future is to *create* it." Here's *your* chance . . .

Here's your chance to begin to create *your* future. You can learn about depression and approach it in a much more realistic way than a "please just fix me" wish. The first thing to understand is that there is no one-size-fits-all "cure" for depression. Instead, there are great tools for *managing* depression, much in the same way you learn to manage other ongoing parts of your life, such as your to-do list or personal finances. The challenge is *learning* and then *using* those tools that can offer a lifetime of relief from depression. Otherwise, it is the equivalent of someone earnestly saying to a physical trainer, "I want to be in great physical shape, but please don't make me exercise!"

Doing what's *easiest*—giving up or just taking a pill—is not the *best* way to overcome depression. I understand the desire to try to take shortcuts when you just want quick relief, but striving to overcome depression isn't about working harder. It's about working *smarter*. This book provides a *realistic* and *scientifically informed* way of thinking about and approaching depression that will help you create a rewarding future.

Michael D. Yapko, PhD
www.yapko.com

Part 1:
Building a Foundation for Success

#1 Learn About Depression: People Educated About Depression Are Much More Likely to Overcome It

Too often, people say, "Just tell me what to do to get out of this depression, Doctor." Unfortunately, there isn't a single treatment or a "best" approach. But there is good reason to be hopeful. There is likely a successful pathway out of depression, but it is up to you to develop this pathway based on a solid understanding of *your* depression.

Depression is a complex experience. It isn't easy to define or describe since each person develops and experiences depression differently. The mental health profession defines depression as a "mood disorder" featuring common symptoms, such as sadness, guilt, a loss of pleasure, sleep disturbance, fatigue, and social withdrawal. However, depression is much more than just your mood and a collection of troublesome symptoms. In fact, depression can reach into and affect virtually every aspect of one's life, from the ability to work, to function as an effective partner and parent, to behave responsibly, to form and maintain positive relationships, to solve problems, and more. Depression exists on many dimensions, not just the one dimension of mood.

Because depression is so complex, there have been many different theories attempting to explain what it is and how it comes about. Some of these theories believe depression is biological, some view it as primarily psychological, and others view it as a social phenomenon. It's like the old tale of the blind men who each touch the elephant in a different place, thus each man has a different description about the elephant's essential features, and no one is able to fully grasp the big picture of what defines an elephant.

Why bother to explore the different viewpoints regarding depression? The simplest most straightforward answer is that your experience of depression is unique to you. No single viewpoint will fully explain all of your experience, and no single viewpoint can provide all of the answers you will need to overcome your depression. What is clear, however, is that when people are well informed about depression—when they know the signs and symptoms, especially their own particular triggers or vulnerabilities, and when they understand the goals and methods of treatment and can participate as an active and knowledgeable partner in the process—they are much more likely to overcome depression. This book can certainly help you acquire useful information, as well as a helpful perspective on your life and how depression affects your life. This book continually emphasizes that there is no one theory that fully explains depression, and there is no single treatment that works well for everyone. Thus, the better you understand depression in general, as well as your individual experience of depression in particular, the more you can weave bits and pieces of information and self-understanding into a successful plan to overcome it.

#2 Depression Can Be a Normal Reaction to Life Stressors

The fact that human beings come equipped with an emotional life can be a blessing or curse, depending on your point of view. Our range of feelings is impressive, but some emotions can be painful and disruptive. While purging yourself of emotions makes for intriguing fictional characters in science fiction shows, in real life, *the more realistic goal is to learn how to manage your feelings skillfully* since they are inevitable. Learning to recognize and even how to direct your feelings in useful ways is a cornerstone of being mentally healthy.

There are countless situations that can occur in one's life that can trigger feelings of grief, despair, anger, resignation, and other such unpleasant but entirely normal feelings. When someone you love dies or leaves you, when you lose a job that has provided you with status or financial security, when your "reason for being" is gone (such as when your children grow up and leave home), when you face rejection, disappointment, betrayal, humiliation, and so many other situations that can hurt you, depression can surface. Such depression is likely to be painful but brief, as it (hopefully) gives way to new understandings and effective actions.

There are two key distinctions between what can be considered a "normal" depression and one that requires active intervention: how bad things get, and for how long. When the experience of depression is so powerful that it warps your view of yourself and your life in negative ways, then your depression is no longer "normal." For example, when depression creeps into your relationships and makes you emotionally distant, hostile, or volatile, when it infects your quality of life with apathy or pessimism and makes life seem a burdensome chore, and these consequences persist in your life for days, which turn into weeks, which turn into months, then your depression requires attention.

When you experience "normal" depression, you get hurt or find yourself facing some painful circumstance or experience emotional pain, you can endure the depression without making bad decisions that make matters even worse, and you gradually "bounce back" over a matter of weeks or months. "Normal" is knowing and *living* the realization that hard times happen, but they don't define the total meaning of your life. Bad things happen, but remember, *good* things happen, too.

#3 No One Overcomes Depression By Declaring Him or Herself a Victim

When you suffer from depression, you tend to feel as though there is nothing you can do about it. It seems to have you in its grip and drains you of any hope that it will ever go away. Energy is at a low point, effort may seem futile, so trying to muster the energy to do something about it can seem overwhelming. It may seem like the only possible course of action is to give up trying to overcome it. Giving up seems especially reasonable when you've tried medications and therapy and who knows what else and none of these have made a dent in your battle against depression.

Giving up is the path of least resistance—it keeps depression going, and it is the ultimate statement of declaring yourself a victim of depression. While that viewpoint is understandable, it makes overcoming depression next to impossible. Recovering from depression is not only possible, but it is *likely*. Most people who suffer from depression do eventually recover. But not every recovery is complete, and not every recovery is free from eventual relapses. It is not a coincidence that those who have higher levels of recovery have a lower likelihood of further episodes. They did some pretty tough work to actively learn about depression, learn about their own individual vulnerabilities or risk factors, and learn the specific skills they'd need to manage these vulnerabilities well.

I urge you to put aside any feelings of hopelessness and helplessness you might have and begin the process of an active recovery. You can lift yourself out of the victim frame of mind and begin to reclaim your life, wiser, less vulnerable, and more determined than ever to make depression a thing of the past. I realize this is easier said than done, but doing what works is rarely 'easy.' I can hold your hand by giving you information, but I can't make you walk. You have to take those steps yourself. You can do this by learning about depression, for the first challenge in overcoming depression is knowing what you're dealing with. And, finally, you can learn about the things you can do *every day* to strengthen yourself against the challenges of life whether they come at you from the outside or from within.

You *can* do this.

#4 Depression Is Not Fated By Genes or Biochemistry

Depression seems to run in families so, understandably, some people form the belief that depression must be caused by faulty genetics, a so-called "depression gene." The field of genetics has made remarkable advances, including mapping the human genome. Has a depression gene been found? *No.* One of the leading geneticists in the United States, Kenneth Kendler, MD, summarized the findings succinctly when he proclaimed there aren't genes that make you depressed, but there are genes that make you vulnerable to depression.

Thus, genetics isn't the area you need to be the most concerned about. Rather, it's the field of epigenetics that is more relevant in your efforts to feel better. Epigenetics is the study of how environmental factors influence genetic expression. Consider the fact that identical twins born with the same genetic makeup can be quite different from each other years later when they have been exposed to different environmental factors.

Think about different family environments. For example, how does growing up with harsh, demanding, emotionally distant parents affect someone's vulnerability to depression? Or, what about perfectionistic parents who make it clear that no matter what you do, it just isn't good enough? Or, the so-called "helicopter" parents who strive to make sure you are always babied and never face frustration or failure that unintentionally leaves you unable to cope with even minor disappointments or adversities? Or, what about those who grew up without parents, or had severely impaired parents who were caught up in drug abuse, alcoholism, or mental illness? The point is that these environments affect whether and how the genes you were born with get expressed in everyday life. In other words, your genes alone are not the culprit of how you feel, but rather how those genes interact with the environment.

Your external environment matters in shaping gene expression. So does your internal environment. Being relaxed and self-accepting influences gene expression in measurable ways that are quite different than being stressed and self-critical or self-destructive. One recent Harvard study showed that just learning to relax changed more than 1,500 genes in just a few weeks! This is an important point for you to understand – genes can be modified by things you do.

You can't change your past, but you can change your environments, both internal and external. You can learn to focus, relax, problem-solve, build a support network, and develop many more such skills that will affect you in positive ways all the way down to the cellular level. *Your genes are not your destiny.*

#5 Depression Can Be a Predominantly Medical or Physical Issue in Some Cases: Getting a Thorough Physical Exam Is a *Great* Idea

Although calling depression a "mental illness" or a "disease" is common, it is too one-dimensional in suggesting that depression is an entirely biologically based phenomenon. But it shouldn't be interpreted that biology is unimportant. In fact, biology can matter *a lot*. There are many medical conditions or diseases where depression is a possible, even likely, consequence. Likewise, there are many drugs, both prescription and street drugs, that can generate depression as a predictable side effect.

Alcohol, as just one example, is a common drug of abuse for people suffering from depression. But alcohol is itself a depressant, and drinking is a prime example of how people make things worse by the way they try to cope with their depression. They drink to help themselves fall asleep, they drink to calm their ever-present anxiety, and they drink "just to escape." Using alcohol to cope is a strategy that *guarantees* the continuation of depression. For people who are depressed or are prone to depression, alcohol is an exceptionally bad drug and should be avoided completely. *Completely.*

One of the very first things, if not *the* first thing you should consider doing if you haven't already done so, is to see your physician if you are suffering from depression. Share your concerns openly about depression with your doctor and have a thorough physical examination. The odds are that there won't be a physical reason for your depression, but the odds mean nothing if it turns out that there is something going on with you that requires medical attention. Physical causes need to be ruled out before treating depression any other way.

The other major reason to get a thorough physical is because depression itself is harmful to your health. The ongoing stress that wears on your body, the significantly higher risk for heart attacks and stroke, and the poorer care of your health are just a few examples of the relationship between depression and your overall physical health.

#6 Depression Does Not Generally Strike "Out of the Blue"

Depression can have a seemingly sudden onset. Sometimes it's for a clear, biological reason, such as an illness or a side effect to a medication regimen. But, most often, this isn't the trigger. Rather, and more typically, some negative event happens, such as someone loses a job, and then he or she becomes depressed. The temptation, of course, is to say that the job loss triggered the depression. That's only partly true. Why is it that some people lose a job and *don't* become depressed? It isn't just the job loss, rather, there is some vulnerability, some risk factor in the person that makes him or her react to a job loss with depression. Perhaps it's the loss of status the job provided, or it's the absence of a life structure ("What do I do if I don't go to work?"), or it's the perception of being rejected and feeling worthless, or it's feeling victimized by an unfair decision to terminate the position, etc. Or, perhaps it's any of the many other possible reasons. The key point is that the situation may be negative, but *it's the view and the handling of the situation that determines whether you are less or more likely to become depressed.*

Sometimes depression isn't caused by external circumstances, like a job loss or the loss of a loved one. Sometimes it appears seemingly out of nowhere, particularly when there isn't any identifiable cause: "My life is going okay, so why am I depressed?" Even in such instances, there is some risk factor at work: it can be any kind of feeling or belief that influences self-awareness and self-judgment. Thoughts such as, "Everything is going great, so why aren't I happy?" or, "I don't deserve to be happy," or, "How can I be okay when there is so much war and destruction in the world?" can easily give rise to depressed feelings. Thoughts can be triggers or risk factors for depression depending on their qualities.

It's essential that you patiently and insightfully learn what your own risk factors for depression are. The things that don't bother other people may bother you (and vice versa). Some examples of risk factors are:

1. The harmful or unrealistic things you tell yourself about other people that make relationships difficult or painful;

2. Emotionally charged life situations you face that you don't know how to handle very well;

3. The places inside yourself where you feel weak and vulnerable and can't trust yourself to do what needs to be done;

4. The difficult feelings you don't know how to identify, manage, or express, and;

5. The ways you don't feel you measure up to how you think you "should" be, whether physically, socially, professionally or in some other area of your life.

There are many possible risk factors for depression and these differ from one person to another. Some of these are physical, psychological, and social. Until you know *your* risk factors well and thereby get the bigger picture of what's going on with your depression, you can too easily believe your depression just struck "out of the blue." That belief then leaves you without any clue as to where to begin your recovery. Trying "anything" just to get some relief can sidetrack you and delay you from pursuing a more sensible, focused personal treatment based on your individual needs. Knowledge of your risk factors is not only important for overcoming depression but also for preventing further episodes. Make your list of risk factors and add to it as you learn about yourself throughout this book. When you know your risk factors, you can start to anticipate when you're in a vulnerable position or a situation that may trigger your depression. Then, you can have skills in place to either avoid the situation if you can, or retrain yourself to think about it differently so you can continue to prevent episodes of depression from recurring.

#7 Depression Has a High Response Rate to Placebo Interventions

When researchers are testing out some new treatment, whether it's a drug, surgical procedure, or something else, they often make use of placebos as a way to compare the effects of the new treatment to no treatment at all. A placebo is an inert substance (or treatment) that appears to be a legitimate treatment but is actually a sham or fake treatment. For example, someone is given a pill he or she is led to believe is an active drug. In fact, it is just a "sugar pill" or some pill that has no actual medicinal value. The so-called "placebo effect" is evident when an inactive substance produces a positive treatment response. In other words, the placebo generates a medical benefit despite the fact that it has no actual medicinal value. How does this happen?

The placebo effect is one of the most researched and controversial yet consistent findings in all of medicine. It also has a negative counterpart, called the "nocebo effect," in which someone expects the drug (or treatment) to hurt rather than help, then that person will react badly to the treatment.

The factor of expectancy largely drives placebo and nocebo effects. In terms of antidepressants, people *expect* to get better from the treatment, so they do. How exactly an expectancy of benefit turns into an actual benefit is still not very well understood. But there is apparently some mechanism by which an expectation translates into a physical response, a mind-body connection that is tapped into by one's beliefs in receiving a likely benefit.

What does this have to do with depression? A lot! Regardless of whatever opinion you might have about antidepressant medications, it is important to know that many studies have been conducted (and were originally not made public) that showed people who responded most dramatically to placebos seemed to also respond best to antidepressants. Furthermore, in comparing placebos directly against antidepressants, the antidepressants generally had a benefit so little beyond the level of a placebo effect that many experts concluded that the side effects and other risks of antidepressants just weren't worth it. In fact, the National Health Service (NHS) in England now has a standard policy to no longer prescribe antidepressants to depression sufferers except in the most severe cases.

Curiously, even drugs that have virtually opposite mechanisms, such as those that *reduce* serotonin concentration in the brain rather than increasing it, still generate the same treatment success rate! Furthermore, other classes of drugs that shouldn't have any effect on depression likewise have a similar level of positive treatment response.

As you will discover, the emphasis of effective treatments for depression is on *action*. Just taking action, even the action of taking a fake drug, generates an improvement in depression symptoms. It seems more sensible, though, to take actions that go beyond stimulating some kind of placebo effect but instead stimulate some *genuine* and long-lasting relief through the acquisition of enduring life-enhancing skills, such as those included in Appendix A. This is what good therapy can do when empowering you to better manage your outlook and mood.

#8 Antidepressants Alone Cannot Solve Your Life's Problems

The use of antidepressant medications to treat depression is currently the most common form of treatment, a tribute to the triumph of marketing over science. Billions of dollars are spent to lead us to believe that depression is a disease and that medications are the best treatment. Most of these medications are prescribed by physicians who are not mental health professionals. Rather, they are general practitioners, cardiologists, obstetricians, endocrinologists, and other non-psychiatric specialists. Physicians are naturally inclined to assume biological causes and therefore provide biological solutions for people's problems. As a result, they are far more likely to prescribe drugs for the problems that people present to them than suggest other approaches. Unfortunately, psychological issues are not generally best treated medically.

Beyond physicians prescribing drugs too often as the sole treatment, what about those times when the biological bias belongs to the *patient*? Should people be given an antidepressant medication simply because they asked for one? The evidence is clear that doctors are more likely to prescribe a drug when the patient requests it. The drug companies' financial investment in advertising to consumers is well rewarded. This is marketing over science.

When so much of depression is rooted in psychological and social factors, a drug simply *cannot* address these. No wonder, then, that drugs have the highest relapse rate of any form of treatment. Just taking a drug alone may be the *simplest* approach but it isn't typically the best approach to overcoming depression. For some people, the drug has a therapeutic benefit even though no one really knows why. Medications do help some people. For many people, the drug (or maybe it's just the *expectation* of the drug) gives them a boost, a sense of being able to overcome their depression. They may start to feel better and then start doing things they need to do to get better.

In the last few years, there has been a growing backlash against antidepressant medications and with good reason. Evidence has come to light that the drug companies have engaged in extremely deceptive practices, deliberately falsifying data in research trials in order to get drugs approved by the government for widespread usage (and exceptionally large profits). They have lied about the safety of the drugs, leading people to believe they are safer than they really are. They have also lied about the effectiveness of the drugs, greatly exaggerating their value while also minimizing their potentially hazardous side effects. The lawsuits are well underway because of the harm many have suffered.

If the drugs were clearly safe and effective, I wouldn't hesitate to recommend them to you, but the issues are complicated, and the therapeutic value of the drugs is not as straightforward as we would like it to be. Too much money—literally billions of dollars—is at stake, and the will of special interest groups has clouded the picture.

Even for those who view drug treatments favorably, they would still have to acknowledge that no drug can identify your personal vulnerabilities, teach you better problem-solving skills, coping skills, and relationship skills. Nor can they help you build a support network, or help with the many things that can make a huge positive difference beyond the drug's effects. Psychotherapy should be a part of any formal treatment plan for this reason. A so-called "combined therapy" of drugs and psychotherapy is generally recommended, but too few people receive such treatments.

The decision regarding whether to take an antidepressant is a complicated one. I urge you to take the time to learn more about this issue before you simply assume you need to be medicated. It *isn't* a "given"; rather, it requires careful consideration.

#9 There Is No Cure for Feelings: Your Mood Has to Be Managed With Insight, Foresight, and *Forever*

If you are capable of having feelings, then you are capable of having depressed feelings as well as *good feelings*. Learning to tell one feeling from another is a developmental process psychologists call "emotional differentiation." It's often the case that people who are vulnerable to depression have a difficult time sorting out their feelings and then knowing what to do with them. In an overgeneral way, the person might say, "I feel bad," without really knowing in what way exactly, thereby preventing taking effective action to address the feeling. So, learning your own individual makeup is an important starting place for eventually learning how to manage your feelings. This is the process of developing insight. If you're human, you're going to have feelings, good and bad, so learning to recognize and respond to them effectively is necessary for your good mental health. Foresight allows you to think ahead and anticipate what you can do preventively based on your insight or self-understanding.

As I said at the beginning of this book, people naturally look for the "depression cure." There is no "cure" for depression simply because there is no "cure" for the inevitable difficulties of life and the range of feelings we all experience and must learn to manage. If you're alive you'll be capable of experiencing depression as well as all the other feelings on the emotional spectrum. So, instead of striving to cure depression, you can strive to learn to *manage* your life by *managing* your triggers for depression and learning to *manage* your depressed feelings if and when they arise. It's the emotional parallel to all the other areas of your life that also have to be managed by you on an ongoing basis. After all, you don't make a bank deposit once and now you're done managing your money. You don't exercise once and now you're done managing your physical health. You don't discipline your child once and now you're done with parenting. These and many other aspects of your life are ongoing and require ongoing handling throughout your lifetime.

It's important to develop the realistic mindset that if you are depressed or are vulnerable to depression it is simply because *everyone* is vulnerable to depression to one degree or another. Whether you stay there and decorate it or move on is up to you and the choices you make. I know that may sound harsh when you're feeling depressed, but I'm here to tell you what you need to know to make a change, not what you might want to hear.

There are essential life skills all people must learn for themselves, such as how to manage your time and manage your moods, just as you have to learn to manage your body (only you know when and how much to eat, or when you need sleep or how much exercise you need to feel good). Waiting for someone else to cure your depression, as if anybody could, misses the fact that no one can do it for you. No one can tell you when you're hungry or need rest, and no one can tell you what you're feeling.

For the rest of your life, managing your feelings will be an ongoing challenge . . . *just as it is for the rest of us*. The goal is to manage them with understanding and skill.

#10 Depression Recurs Because Life Recurs

One of the things that research reveals about depression is that it is recurrent, that is, it may go away spontaneously and then come back again, a phenomenon called a "relapse." Each episode of depression you experience can increase the chances of more recurrent episodes if left untreated. Many mental health professionals think that getting people out of depression isn't as much a challenge as it is to help them prevent relapses.

Why are depression sufferers vulnerable to relapses? The conventional wisdom in the field has suggested that this is just the nature of depression, that it is a disorder that features relapses as one of its basic features. I have developed a different viewpoint about this issue. I don't think it's depression that is necessarily recurrent. Rather, I think it is *life* that is recurrent. By that I mean that none of us escape life's inevitable adversities. The people we love die, the friends we cherish move away, the jobs we rely on get lost in a budget crunch, the new car that is our source of pride gets smashed the first week we own it, our kids get their faces tattooed and their bodies pierced, and on and on. All of us face these challenges in life, but most people take them in stride and bounce back and still manage to find that life is generally pretty good.

But, if you don't have the resilience skills to manage adversities and bounce back, then each time you face an adversity, however big or small it might be, you can easily sink back into depression. The term "resiliency" means an ability to recover quickly and efficiently from some setback, and given how many setbacks we all face in our lives—including disappointments, rejections, betrayals, losses, illnesses, and more—it is critically important to develop the skill of making sure you don't define yourself by the adversities you suffer. That means understanding that tough things happen in life, *but that's not all that life is about.* This is why it's so important to strive for balance in your life by actively seeking out good times and good people to counterbalance the stressors and tough times. Otherwise, it's too easy to wallow in the bad times and convince yourself that life is a heavy burden.

Life isn't one-dimensional: bad things happen, but good things happen, too. It helps to notice them when they happen. I encourage my clients to actively keep a list of when they notice those good things so that their focus can start to shift from negative to positive. It's a worthy goal to go out of your way to make even small good things happen *a lot.*

#11 No Amount of Motivation Makes Up for a Lack of Skill, and No Amount of Skill Makes Up for a Lack of Motivation

One of the least helpful perspectives that some people take is that depressed people must *want* to be depressed. They observe, often correctly, that the depressed person does little or nothing to help him or herself, ignoring even obvious things to do that would be helpful. They conclude, therefore, that the person must enjoy depression and perhaps even benefit from it when other people begin to cater to them and show them extra concern or even take over some or all of their responsibilities. But in adopting that cynical perspective, they miss the fact that the core features of depression are the feelings of helplessness and hopelessness that drive the apathy and lead to simply giving up and doing nothing. It's not that people want to be depressed; rather, they've *resigned* themselves to depression.

I'm speaking directly to the issue of motivation. People seem to think that if you're properly motivated then you'll somehow, as if by magic, have the necessary skills. The saying, "Where there's a will, there's a way," says it directly enough—if you want it badly enough, you'll do it. So, even when people say things such as, "I really want to do *x*," whatever *x* might happen to be, but they're not doing it, they may be told they "must not *really* want it." It's as if motivation alone is supposed to be enough to succeed, but it's not. No amount of motivation can make up for not having the necessary abilities to accomplish the desired goal. *It doesn't matter how motivated you are to watch the sunset. If you face east you're not going to see it!*

Too often, people don't realize that the reason they're not getting somewhere in their lives isn't because of a lack of motivation. It's because the way they're going about doing things just isn't working and they need to *do something else*. But, instead of figuring out or asking someone else what else to do that would be helpful, they just give up, assuring continued frustration, feelings of failure, and depression. It's so important to understand this point: If you don't know what to do to get on a path of success, talk to someone who does. You don't have to (and *can't*) know everything. You just have to know where to get help for those times you get stuck. Greater motivation isn't going to help but a new approach to the problem will. Develop a plan for what to do when you are stuck and have no idea what to do, and save yourself the frustration and self-criticism, since these don't help you solve the problem. When you don't know what to do, seek assistance from someone who does, someone who can help fill in the gaps in your knowledge and experience that can help you approach your goal with greater understanding and skill so you can succeed.

The reverse is equally true, of course: No amount of skill will make a difference if you're not motivated to use whatever skills you may have. Far too many people squander their natural gifts because they get lost in their feelings. Having skill without focus and motivation is simply opportunity wasted. Discovering your natural gifts and learning how to develop and use them in effective ways is a challenge everyone faces, and rising to that challenge is one of the things that gives our lives meaning.

#12 Eat Better and Exercise Regularly

No doubt easier said than done, it's a worthy goal to want to provide your body with the best nutrition you can give it and keep it running stronger and healthier by getting regular exercise. Most people responding to surveys on these subjects claim they strive to eat healthy and exercise but also admit to being inconsistent about their nutrition and exercise. *Some* inconsistency is inevitable and should be accepted without guilt and recriminations. But just following your feelings, *impulsive* feelings, can easily lead to bad decisions you'll later regret. Thinking *beyond* the moment is critically important if you are to succeed in the endeavor of eating better and exercising more.

While there is no specific diet that has been shown to improve depression, a balanced diet of natural rather than processed foods that is high in nutrients (minerals, vitamins, carbohydrates, and protein) is essential to your physical health. Your diet provides the building blocks for your brain chemistry, metabolism, *every* bodily function. It's harder to feel good mentally, of course, if you're feeling lousy physically.

Exercise in particular has been studied heavily in terms of its effects on depression. There is plenty of good research to show that regular exercise lifts your mood and keeps it elevated. People report as much a reduction in their depression symptoms from exercising as they report from taking antidepressants. That's great news, because it means there's something almost anyone can do that will have a benefit and without negative side effects. An additional benefit is that people who exercise regularly have a much lower depression relapse rate than if they only take medications.

There hasn't been any one form of exercise that has been shown to be significantly better than another. Walking, running, bicycling, weight lifting, just about anything you can do that you feel good doing will make a helpful difference. Start slowly, build up slowly, and do what you enjoy.

Why does exercise help so much? There are different views on this. Some claim it's because exercise kick-starts the brain with the release of "feel good" brain chemicals. Some claim it's because people feel empowered by getting physically stronger. Others claim it's because it gets you out of negative ruminations and self-absorption and shifts your attention to the positive benefits of exercise.

I think these are all likely to be true and would add one more possibility: Depressed people generally have "low-frustration tolerance" and tend to give up easily if things don't improve right away when they expend some effort. Exercise is an area where the gains are clear and pretty rapid: You could only walk a block last week and this week you're walking several.

Exercise feels good, it's good for you on every level, and it's free… so go for it!

#13 Get Some Good Sleep

Sleep issues in particular represent the most common complaint associated with depression. It is no surprise that the second most common symptom of depression is fatigue. It's hard to feel good when you're tired, and it's hard to pursue pleasurable activities alone or with others when you're exhausted all the time.

Unfortunately, physicians typically prescribe a sleep medication if a patient reports a sleep disturbance instead of inquiring about what else might be going on in the patient's life and suggesting a more natural and empowering way to develop better sleeping habits. Sleep drugs can make a bad problem worse if they're not handled carefully.

The most common sleep disturbance is some form of insomnia. It might be *initial insomnia*, affecting the ability to fall asleep. Or, it might be *middle insomnia*, where you fall asleep for two or three hours then wake up and have difficulty falling back to sleep. Or, it might be *terminal insomnia*, where you wake up two or three hours before you intend to and then can't fall back asleep. Terminal insomnia seems to be the most common form of insomnia related to depression. Initial and middle insomnia seem to be more closely related to anxiety.

Too often people use alcohol to manage the anxiety, saying, "I like to have a drink or two before bed, because it helps me fall asleep." It may help you fall asleep, but it aggravates depression and also practically guarantees middle insomnia, that is, waking up two or three hours later and then having difficulty falling back asleep once you've metabolized the alcohol. *Alcohol is a bad drug if you're depressed* for many reasons, and its negative effect on sleep is just another one.

The most common reason for insomnia is the tendency to ruminate, repetitively thinking about the things that bother you, spinning them around and around, and agitating yourself in the process. As you do so, you release stress hormones that mobilize alertness at a time when you want to sleep. Thus, learning to relax and focus on the moment when you want to sleep is the goal rather than going to bed and focusing on problems. The value of mindful meditation, self-hypnosis, visualization, yoga and other similar focusing and relaxing processes are extremely effective in helping with sleep issues and are far safer and far more personally empowering than taking sleep drugs. These are focusing skills worth developing.

If you have trouble falling asleep and need a positive and healthy alternative to taking sleep medication, I have produced a focusing session for improving sleep called *Sleeping Soundly* that is available as a download for purchase on my website (www.yapko.com). Good sleep is critically important to feeling good. Sleep is physically and mentally restorative, it regulates the release of certain neurotransmitters and hormones, it helps consolidate learning, and it powerfully affects our overall quality of functioning. For some people, resolving their sleep issue is enough to reduce their depression given the domino effect of good sleep.

Part 2:
Key Personal Skills Necessary to Manage Depression

#14 Life Is Ambiguous

It is the most natural thing to want to ask "why." "Why is this happening?" "Why do I feel this way?" "Why do I do these things that work against me?" Why, why, why?

Asking *why* may be motivated out of a basic human need to understand and thereby possibly have some control over whatever is going on in your life. Unfortunately, there are too many things that happen in life for reasons we don't currently understand or may *never* understand. Not all questions are answerable in a meaningful way, and not all events can be traced to an identifiable cause.

This is what the phrase "life is ambiguous" means: things happen in life that may directly affect you, *but you don't really know why they're happening*. Yet, you reflexively strive to make some sense of them and explain them to yourself: "This is happening *because* . . ." This is the process of interpreting ambiguous events.

Your interpretations are called "projections." You project onto the ambiguous situation an explanation you made up that provides you with a reason: "The reason he didn't call me back is because he doesn't like or respect me," or, "The reason I didn't get the job is because I'm so lousy at job interviews," or "The reason she turned me down for a date is because she thinks I'm a loser."

There is plenty of research that shows that people who are vulnerable to depression respond to ambiguity differently than people who aren't as vulnerable to depression. Depression typically leads people to make negative projections, meaning, they will interpret ambiguous or unclear situations in ways that hurt them when the interpretations are unfounded. Look at the above examples again.

Unless you ask or do further research, you don't know why he didn't call you back, or why you didn't get the job, or why she turned you down for a date. Instead, we have a habit of jumping to conclusions—filling in the blanks—and then we make the mistake of actually believing that our hurtful conclusions are true.

The key skill that can save you a lifetime of bad feelings is to first learn how to recognize when a situation or interaction is ambiguous and then train yourself to get comfortable saying, "I don't know why," instead of making up or projecting something that hurts you unnecessarily when there's no evidence it's true.

Learn to gather facts and evidence whenever possible. Too many ambiguous things happen every day for which there are no clear explanations, but gathering facts and evidence is a good first step before simply believing something to be true that may not be at all true. This is so important if you are to be a more critical thinker and thereby make better decisions.

Ambiguity invites projection, but it's an invitation you can refuse.

#15 Your Mood Affects Your Memory and How You Recall Your Personal History

One of the emerging and fascinating areas of research concerns the relationship between mood and various cognitive processes, such as memory, learning, and problem solving. Depression negatively affects these processes, as well as others. But, in trying to recover from depression, it is often the case that a person's view of his or her own personal history, as he or she recalls it, is a major obstacle to feeling better.

When people feel bad, the effect on their recall is to essentially filter their memories through their bad mood. So, depressed people are far more likely to remember only negative events in their lives and report only these when asked about their personal history, perhaps by a psychotherapist or physician. How negative does a person's history have to be for that person to stay on a depression pathway for years or even decades later?

This is a delicate topic, for there may have been all kinds of bad things that have happened in your life, and that is truly terrible. While no one can change what has already happened in his or her life, it becomes an important step in overcoming depression to recognize that even people with horrible histories have also had good things happen. These are a few simple but realistic examples: you got a fun toy at a gift exchange at an elementary school Christmas party; you did better on a spelling test than you expected to; you found money in the street and bought yourself an ice cream; you discovered a talent you didn't know you had; you had a teacher you really liked who liked you, too. You can't change your history, but your can change which aspects of it you choose to focus upon.

Go out of your way to find many examples in your life of good things happening even during bad times and start to expand your view of your history as "all bad." Starting a list and making a point of adding further examples of something good that happened to you whenever you suddenly recall another good one can be a great help to you. Unless you directly challenge the one-dimensional perspective that weighs you down, you may too easily lead yourself to believe that you are always going to be a "prisoner of the past." It's easier to deal with and come to terms with *specific* hard times than it is to *globally* declare your whole life an enduring trauma. It's a distortion of the facts to do so.

Always remember: *You're more than your history.*

#16 The Past Does Not Predict the Future

Each of us relates to time differently. Some people "live in the past," some are "here and now" types, and others are focused on "what's next?". How you relate to time has a significant influence on the kinds of problems you are likely to develop. For examples, impulsive behaviors, such as excessive drinking or casual unprotected sex, clearly reflect a "right now" orientation, while anxiety is a typical and obvious consequence of the worry that the future holds harm of one kind or another in store for you.

Depression, on the other hand, is more of a past-oriented phenomenon. It is typical for depression sufferers to focus on past hurts of all kinds: rejections, failures, betrayals, humiliations, and so on. Even when thinking about the future, the predictions are still rooted in the past: "I'll *never* be happy because I never *have been*"; "I'll *never* have a good relationship because I've never *had one*"; "I'll *never* be able to succeed because I never *have been* able to succeed"; and, probably the most popular one of all, *"I won't be happy until my parents treat me better when I was a kid!"* How convoluted is that?

While using your past (or even your present) experiences as a reference point to make predictions about your future is entirely understandable, it is also *a reliable way to stay stuck* in the depressing perception that expending any effort to help yourself is futile. This is the main pathway to the "why bother?" victim mentality that is the badge of depression.

Recovery from depression is possible when you shift your focus from the unchangeable past to the opportunities of the future. You can begin to define more clearly *in action terms* what you want (rather than only saying what you *don't* want, as in, "I just don't want to be depressed"), and develop and follow realistic plans for making these things happen. Unfortunately, this is where things often break down for people, because they typically know what they want. It's more likely they just don't know the specific steps to follow in order to get where they want to go. That's why people so often ended up trying and trying again, but they simply do more of the same thing that hasn't worked. Try again, but *do something different*! That's why it's so critically important to talk to people, especially a skilled psychotherapist, who can help you take deliberate and effective steps to make sure your future isn't just more of the same.

You can learn what you need to learn to succeed, you can develop new and better ways of achieving the things you want to achieve, and you can create a future for yourself that is better than the past has been. To do that, you'll need a sensible and detailed plan and the willingness to follow that plan even when you might have your doubts. Having the guidance and support of someone who knows the road you're following can make all the difference in the world in terms of your future success. Always keep in mind that just because you haven't done it before doesn't mean you won't be able to in the future. After all, *the future hasn't happened yet.*

#17 Your Feelings Can Deceive You

Learning to manage your depression skillfully means developing a revised relationship with your feelings, especially your depressed ones. That revision begins the moment you understand the fact that your feelings can lie to you. They can lead you to misread situations, distort your perceptions, form erroneous conclusions, react badly, mismanage your relationships, avoid taking sensible and timely actions, and on and on.

Your feelings can also tell you the truth sometimes. This is where the skill in managing feelings well is to be found. When your feelings can tell you the truth and your feelings can deceive you, *how do you know* which feelings to follow and which ones to override?

Giving this important question careful thought is the first step toward developing the ability to put just enough distance between you and your feelings to begin to develop control over them. Instead of just being a "raw nerve" and instantly reacting emotionally, you can learn to observe and evaluate your feelings, recognizing that *sometimes* they are out of line with what's actually going on. You can learn to contain and manage your feelings, because if you don't, you can too easily get wrapped up in them and they will work against attaining your goals in some situation. This is a skill psychologists call "emotional self-regulation." *You're more than your feelings.* Somehow, though, far too many people have given their feelings a special sacred status they really don't deserve. They say, "Don't question my feelings!" or declare, "I'm entitled to my feelings," or they simply follow their feelings even when their feelings are leading them off a cliff.

It changes your relationships with others for the better when those who are close to you have the freedom to *respectfully* question your feelings. After all, they may be your feelings, but they may be feelings that arise from errors in perception. If you take the defensive posture, "Don't question my feelings!" you put up a barrier that can harm the relationship by closing off honest communication and also keep you from possibly reconsidering the matter and taking a better position. Until you're willing to entertain other possibilities, it's too easy to get locked into a viewpoint that isn't helpful to the circumstances and may be derived from faulty understandings. You may be right, as it turns out, but you might not be, and you won't know until you explore the issue more thoughtfully.

Likewise, it improves your view of yourself when you are able to question your own feelings. Maybe they are accurately reflecting what's going on but maybe they aren't. Further fact-finding can help make things clearer, as can choosing to delay reacting or taking some course of action until you've had a chance to put some emotional distance between yourself and the decision to be made or the action to be taken.

It bears repeating, *you're more than your feelings*. That's an insight worth taking into your heart and mind.

#18 Do Not Believe Yourself: Reality Test

Human beings are story machines. It is fundamentally human to create stories to explain the meaning of life events around us, from how we all got here to what happens after we're gone. We generate stories about why people do the things they do and say the things they say. Many of these are stories we tell ourselves about ourselves: who we think we are, why we think we're this way, what we think our lives are about, what we think we're capable of, how we think people should treat us, what we think we deserve, what we can do to and with our bodies, and on and on.

Some stories we tell ourselves create possibilities and open us up to life-enhancing experiences. Other stories close us down and make us miserable. What a difference to think, "Life is an adventure to be lived to the fullest" compared to thinking, "Life is a burden and then you die."

One of the most troublesome patterns of depression is called the "internal orientation." It refers to the focus on one's own thoughts and feelings and using them as the reference point for making meaning of life events and for making decisions. For example, when someone says or even just implies, "I don't feel that way so *neither should you*," or, 'This is how I see it so *you should see it that way too*," he or she is using his or her own feelings as the determinant of how others should feel. To use your own frame of reference to interpret others' actions or make important decisions is potentially dangerous: other people may not feel the way you feel or care about what you care about. Depressed moods can distort your perceptions of others' motives and actions in a negative direction. For example, you can easily misinterpret someone's teasing you as a personal attack when it was just intended to be playful. Furthermore, depressed mood can distort your decision-making process by injecting an unwarranted pessimism into it with predictably bad consequences ("why bother?").

It is one thing to be aware of your thoughts and feelings, but it is quite another to allow yourself to believe these thoughts and feelings accurately represent the world around you and, especially, the other people inhabiting that world. Given how easy it is for *all* of us to think things and make the mistake of believing ourselves, it is critically important to evolve the skill called "reality testing." Reality testing is about getting out of yourself (your internal orientation) long enough to find out whether what you're thinking and feeling is supported by the available facts. For example, instead of assuming you know what this person thinks, it would be wise to ask. You might find out you were correct, but you might also find out you were way off in your perceptions. As another example, you might assume no one would hire you, but you won't know that until you put in the job application. Predicting failure and then not trying, as if you know your prediction is right, reinforces depression. It misses the chance to find out from sources *outside yourself* whether you were right.

If you want to overcome depression, it will be enormously helpful if you learn to reality test—gather facts and test your perceptions—rather than reacting to your depressed beliefs about yourself and others as if they're true. Maybe they are, maybe they aren't, but you won't know if you never bother to actually find out. This skill is not only vital to getting out of depression, but it's also vital to preventing relapses.

#19 Learn to Think More Flexibly and Push Yourself to Generate Multiple Viewpoints

One of the hallmarks of depression is a pattern called "cognitive rigidity." Mental health professionals use the term to describe someone who is so stuck in his or her viewpoint that he or she simply can't see any other way of viewing the situation or issue. It is a powerful factor in causing and maintaining depression when someone is "locked into" a self-damaging or depressing perspective. Here's how it works: Some event happens (for example, you call someone, leave a message, but receive no return call) and you instantly form an interpretation or conclusion about what it means to you ("no one cares about me"), and your critical thinking stops there and goes no further. Given how often a depressed person's interpretation or conclusion is hurtful to him or her, he or she is now "stuck" with this perception. It feels bad, adding to the depression.

Consider how often you may tell yourself hurtful ("I'm such an idiot!") or self-limiting ("I can't possibly do that!") things you *simply accept as true* about yourself. Why don't these change? Rigidity. Why don't you go out of your way to challenge such statements and refuse to buy into them? Rigidity.

Making a snap judgment or jumping to a conclusion that is harmful to you in one way or another is an essential target for helping yourself out of depression and preventing future relapses. The skill that can make all the difference in the world is to generate *at least* three different *plausible* explanations for an event: "Maybe that person acted this way because of *this* . . . or maybe it was because of *that* . . . or possibly it was because of something else going on I can't even guess at." In the example above, maybe your friend hasn't called you back because he/she hasn't received your message yet, or maybe your friend has been too busy to stop and respond and will do so when he/she has the time, or maybe the message got erased, or maybe your friend just doesn't want to talk right now. When you generate multiple viewpoints, it paves the way to ask, "Well then, which one is it?" Maybe there's a way to find out, and maybe there isn't. You may have to just *tolerate the uncertainty* of not knowing. This is the *ambiguity* of life events I spoke of earlier. The goal is to keep from instantly getting attached to a single viewpoint for which there is no evidence that unnecessarily hurts you in the process.

Practice looking at routine events from as many different viewpoints as you possibly can. Pick at least three events each day that were pretty mundane, meaning, they were no big deal for you to manage emotionally. How many different theories can you generate as to why things happened the way they did?

Someone wise once said, "A conclusion is what you reach when you're tired of thinking." There's *some* truth to that observation that's worth thinking about.

#20 Learn to Think Critically and in Greater Detail

The amount of information available to us on just about any topic is both amazing and overwhelming. Google and all the other Internet search engines let us find things in an instant. How does this common technology change the way we use our minds? People used to value and store information in their memories for the sake of being informed. They valued education for the sake of being educated. Now, people ask, "Why do I need to know that? If I want that information, I can Google it." Our "smart phones" have become an external hard drive for our brains, allowing us to have only general knowledge and use technology to acquire specifics only as we need them. There is no doubt that there are obvious benefits to the advent of technology, but there are consequences evolving for us in social and educational terms that we can't even predict yet. I don't think it's a coincidence that the rates of depression continue to rise as we rely more and more on technology.

Here's why: there is a style of thinking associated with depression that falls right into the "Why do I have to know that?" mentality. It's called a "global cognitive style", and it refers to an over-general style of thinking. It's what leads someone to go through a painful breakup with a boyfriend/girlfriend and *globally* say, "Men!" or "Women!" with anger and disgust, as if all men or women are the same. It's what leads someone to go through a bad experience and *globally* say, "*Life* is so unfair!" rather than, "That was a tough time." Do you see the difference between a single example and an overgeneralization? It's critically important that you do, otherwise you unintentionally make problems bigger and harder to solve instead of smaller and easier to solve.

Comedian Lily Tomlin said, "I always wanted to be someone. Now I think I should have been more specific." It's a funny line and highlights the hazards of thinking in over-general terms. You can't solve *specific* problems in a *general* way nor can you learn a new specific skill in a general way.

The vitally important skill of critical thinking—evaluating the merits and qualities of information—is directly related to thinking in greater detail in specific situations. Only by asking for specifics can you discover whether some information you're given is well founded or some plan is plausible and has a reasonable chance of actually working in the way you'd like.

Consider the clear example of politics. Candidates typically say things that strike the nerve of religion or patriotism for voters, yet they provide no specifics as to how they would actually translate their over-general position into a detailed, effective domestic or international policy. For a voter to get "turned on" by the emotional appeal and miss that the whole thing falls apart when you ask the candidate for the details reflects a lack of critical thinking on the part of the voter. It's the political equivalent of getting an email from some former general in some obscure country that says you can be a full partner in a $50 million deal to transfer hidden funds if you'll just send your name, social security number, and bank account number to him. Please *don't*.

Critical thinking means asking questions, locking down the details, assessing credibility, looking for any exceptions to the general rule, and evaluating the plausibility of plans. Instead of just believing someone or even just believing yourself, train yourself to be a critical thinker. Be careful not to over-generalize from one experience, identify counter-examples to the principle or philosophy under consideration, and get the details you need to make sensible and informed decisions that you'll still feel good about later. Critical thinking provides an avenue for preventing regrets.

While this book provides many ideas and helpful possibilities, it is not detailed enough to address or help with all the many issues and patterns associated with something as complex as depression. Pursuing more specific and detailed help through further suggested readings and through personal-growth-oriented work will be essential. Appendix B provides some suggested readings that include many of the kinds of skill-building exercises that are included in Appendix A. Helping you approach these with a better foundation of knowledge and insight is the goal of this book.

#21 You Have More Personal Resources Than You May Realize

When you're feeling down and struggling just to get through the day, it's hard to feel resourceful. You can get lost in the feelings of worthlessness and victimization and, at such emotional times, trying to locate any creativity or strength within yourself may just seem close to impossible.

What does "resourceful" mean? Being resourceful means having inner abilities to tap into that can help you manage some difficult situations, people, or your own feelings more effectively. Resourcefulness further means having the ability to reach inside yourself and bring forth some words and actions that will greatly improve the outcome in meeting the challenges you face. *Resourcefulness serves some greater objective.*

You have heard on the news so many times how someone is just driving along, minding his or her own business, and comes upon an accident that just happened. He or she sees someone trapped in a burning car and just springs into action, pulling the person to safety. Later, he or she is declared a "hero." And what do such people almost invariably say? "I'm no hero. I just did what anybody would do." It may sound like modesty, but it's actually how such people tend to really feel. The point is, you don't really know what you're capable of until you face some challenge and strive to rise to meet it. The real heroes are able to set aside their fears and doubts and keep their focus on the objective, whether it's to pull someone from a burning car or simply handle a rude teenager.

In the above example, the resourcefulness is generated by an unusual and urgent external circumstance. A key point to highlight: you also have inner resources, strengths, and skills to call upon in far less-dramatic life examples that still require you to act with wisdom and courage each and every day. You can build your successes in life and your self-esteem by recognizing these resources in yourself and learning how to use them well.

In the popular 2007 movie, *Evan Almighty*, starring Steve Carell and Morgan Freeman and directed by Tom Shadyac, God appears in the humble disguise of a restaurant worker and speaks to a woman who is confused by and ashamed of her husband's seemingly erratic behavior. Her husband feels compelled to follow God's private command to him to "build an ark" despite his personal doubts about his own sanity and the shame he feels caused by the public ridicule that follows. In an effort to help her find compassion for her husband, God asks her, "If someone prays for patience, you think God gives them patience? Or does he give them the opportunity to be patient? If he prayed for courage, does God give him courage, or does he give him opportunities to be courageous?" The wisdom of the point is clear: situations, especially challenging ones, provide you with *an opportunity* to behave with skill and integrity.

Being resourceful means *responding to the demands of the situation,* often *overriding your feelings of fear or doubt* in order to do so. You'll be amazed with the strengths you find in yourself when you take the time to find them in the service of some greater objective. This is one aspect of what I mean when I say, "You're more than your feelings." You don't have to *have* confidence or courage. You just have to be willing to *act* confidently and courageously when you face difficulty.

#22 You Have More Control Than You May Realize

How you perceive and manage the issue of "control" will have a profound influence on your life, which directly shapes your overall outlook and general mood. You can mishandle situations that become depressing if you try to control situations you can't or, conversely, don't exert control in situations in which you could.

Control refers to a capacity to influence. Having "control" means having the power to influence what happens, either in whole or in part. Psychologists use the term "locus of control" to describe where someone places the power in a given situation. An "internal locus of control" means you believe you have the ability to influence what happens. Conversely, an "external locus of control" means you think the power is elsewhere, somewhere outside yourself.

The problem is, where the control lies in a given situation can seem quite ambiguous to you. This naturally invites projections, or interpretations, about where the control is, paving the way for errors in judgment. Unfortunately, depression sufferers regularly make the error of *underestimating* how much control they have in a circumstance, reflecting the pattern of an external locus of control. This is what gives rise to declaring oneself a victim and simply giving up when, in fact, there is more that can be done to affect the eventual outcome. People don't give up because they like or are comfortable with their depression, as exasperated others sometimes suggest. Rather, they give up because they genuinely believe there is nothing they can do about it.

There's a model of depression called "learned helplessness" that has relevance. Researchers would expose people to unpleasant things they could not escape. Subjects learned that any effort to escape was futile and soon simply gave up trying to escape the noxious stimulus and despairingly resigned themselves to it. Next, conditions were changed so that people *could* escape the noxious stimulus, but based on their previous experience, they *didn't even try* to escape, and this resignation over-generalization was termed "learned helplessness."

The goal isn't to generally have either an internal or external locus of control. Rather, the goal is to read each situation you face accurately. Sometimes you will have an external locus of control because the power is indeed outside of you. Other times you will have an internal locus of control because you really do have the power to influence what happens.

There's another distinction to make that can be helpful to you. If you can do something positive to help change the circumstances, you're exerting what psychologists call "primary control." For example, getting yourself transferred to a different project manager when you don't get along with yours is a primary control strategy. You're changing the troublesome circumstances. Sometimes, though, such a change simply isn't possible. When you can't change the circumstances, the goal then is to *strive to change your reaction to the circumstances.* This is called a "secondary control" strategy. It requires flexibility to adopt a new perspective, and this reflects a life skill worth developing. After all, a lot of life involves adjusting to circumstances you didn't ask for. Thus, it's ideal if you can adjust your reaction to the circumstance without unnecessary suffering generated by how you wish things were, delaying you from adjusting well to how things actually are.

It can help to take the time to identify all the factors that will determine the outcome in some situation you face and then assess whether you have full, partial, or no control over these variables. When you get a clearer sense of how much control you have overall, it can help you to decide whether you're going to focus on changing the circumstances or your reactions to the circumstances. Either way, you have more control than you might have realized.

#23 There Is a Danger in Thinking Too Much

One of the most troublesome patterns associated with depression is a coping style called "rumination." Rumination means spinning around the same thoughts over and over again. Ruminative thinking isn't progressive—it's repetitive—and when negative thoughts are continually being spun around and around, there are direct symptomatic consequences. These include higher levels of anxiety, more symptoms of depression (especially insomnia), higher levels of substance abuse (including eating too much comfort food, taking drugs, and drinking too much alcohol), and a reduction in the ability to engage in effective problem solving. Rumination *isn't* a good approach to solving problems. It's hard to build confidence in yourself if you don't see yourself as generally effective in meeting life's challenges.

The interesting thing is that when you interview ruminators about their ruminating, they think they *are* problem solving. They think they are doing something useful by engaging in seemingly endless analysis of their feelings or endless guessing at others' feelings or motives. However, instead of giving rise to meaningful action, it's just useless spinning.

The therapies that unwittingly encourage rumination can easily make matters worse by promoting more and deeper analysis *at the expense of taking effective action.* It is not a coincidence that the therapies that have the highest treatment success rates for depression all encourage taking action rather than spending more time analyzing why you feel that way. They say, in essence, "Okay, so you feel that way. Now what should you *do* about it?" This push for action is termed "behavioral activation" by psychologists and is considered a cornerstone of good therapy for depression.

There are therapists who will encourage a practice called "journaling," a process of writing about your thoughts, feelings, and experiences. Journaling can definitely be helpful in promoting greater self-awareness and self-expression. But to a ruminator, journaling can simply become ruminating in writing.

If there's such a thing as a cure for rumination, it's action. The goal is to take *timely and effective action*, not just any action. Circumstances define what is timely, for sometimes it will need to be an immediate action you take, and other times you may have days, weeks, or even months to decide what action to take. The actions you take must be thoughtful and sensible and stand a good chance of improving matters, not just doing something merely for the sake of doing something. This requires a thoughtful consideration of this key question: When is it useful analysis, and when is it useless rumination? I'll answer the question for you: If it doesn't lead to timely and effective action, it's useless rumination.

#24 There Is a Danger in Thinking Too Little

As mentioned previously, jumping to conclusions without the facts and adopting a single perspective without considering any other possible viewpoints are two reliable pathways into feeling bad when those conclusions and perspectives are incorrect and hurtful. There are at least two others as well: *Being too self-unaware* and thereby putting yourself in situations that are damaging to you, and *not exercising foresight* and thereby walking into vulnerable situations where harm to you could have been prevented with just a little forethought.

Self-awareness isn't just a lightweight "pop psychology" term. It's an important means of making good decisions based on self-understanding. Without it, people can too easily put themselves into situations where they really don't belong, situations that require things of them that are not a part of their nature that lead to a "rough ride."

As a prime example, consider people who simply don't have the character or temperament to be effective parents. They're hampered by their self-absorption, lack of tolerance, poor or inability to express love, violent temper, cluelessness or selfishness about what it means to be a role model, and any other number of serious flaws that should tell them that parenting is simply not for them. Instead, they thoughtlessly have kids and then the kids end up suffering the consequences because their parents didn't have the means or temperament to provide for them in a positive way. Why shouldn't someone realize they're not "good parent material" *before* they have kids? That same person may be wonderful in other ways, just not for being a parent. That requires self-awareness and self-acceptance.

Choosing relationships, careers, and every other important life decision you can make needs to be done with careful thought if you are to live well with your life choices. That includes the forethought to anticipate what will be required of you, the demands you'll face, and the insight to know whether you can actually do those things at all or at least without it draining you and leaving you miserable. It's important to be able to use self-awareness to promote forethought: "I'm okay with these kinds of people but not with those kinds." "I'm okay with this kind of work environment, but I'm not okay with that kind."

The goal is to recognize and use your gifts, and to honor and make the best use of who and what you are. Living life on a moment-to-moment basis makes that impossible. Developing self-understanding and thinking ahead are vitally important skills to counteract the dangers of thinking too little.

#25 Your Unrealistic Expectations Can Set You Up to Be Let Down

If you were to ask the leading marital researchers what single factor most predicts marital satisfaction, they'd likely say, "How well your spouse lives up to your expectations. If your partner does what you think he or she should do, then you're happy. Likewise, if your partner doesn't do what you think he or she should, then you're unhappy."

Isn't this how we judge nearly *everything*? If the restaurant, movie, book, job-performance review, plumbing repair, surgery, *whatever*, lives up to your expectations, then you're satisfied. The key question is, how do you know whether your expectations are *realistic?*

The "internal orientation" discussed in #18: "Don't Believe Yourself: Reality Test," is a culprit here. You form an idea as to how you think things should be or how someone should behave, and then you find out, probably the hard way, that others had a different idea about how things "should" be.

I sometimes show a cartoon in the trainings I conduct for mental health professionals that features a man and a woman sitting together on the couch. The woman looks pretty unhappy, and the caption reads, "If you really loved me, you'd win the lottery." She apparently has no idea that winning the lottery isn't based on how much you love someone. But by having that unrealistic expectation, she makes herself pretty miserable. It's just half a step away from much more common examples: *If you really loved me, you'd buy me nice jewelry. If you really respected me, you'd give me the raise in salary. If you really cared about me, you'd commit to marrying me.* The internal orientation says, in essence,

"Here's how I see it, so that's how it should be." It misses the fact that organizations, institutions, and people may have a different agenda that have little or nothing to do with your expectations.

There's not only a treatment opportunity here, but also an opportunity for prevention. It would be wise to give some thought to the specifics of what you want to say and the specifics of what you expect in response *before* you walk into a meeting with your manager, *before* you confront your teen about some bad behavior, *before* you make a demand on a friend, or *before* you raise a serious topic with your partner. Then ask yourself, "Here's what I expect from this interaction, but what if he or she reacts differently than I hope or expect?" Asking yourself how you know whether your expectations are realistic *before* you get into the situation can frequently save you from being blindsided. By asking, you might realize you have no idea whether your expectations are realistic since you don't really know the person or organization well enough to know what he, she, or they are likely to think, feel, or do. *You simply can't make good predictions on the basis of no substantive information.* If you realize you don't know enough to make a good prediction, it will save you from getting too attached to a wish or an expectation for which there is no plausible basis. Even if your predictions become good ones, however, there's no assurance you'll be right *this* time.

#26 Everyone Needs a Code to Live By: Your Values Help Define You

From the time we are born, we are socialized by our families, schools, religious training, and by the larger society of which we are all inevitably a part. Socialization means being shaped into believing and behaving in ways that are consistent with what others, especially our significant others, expect of us. Over time, we absorb deeply held values that we've come to think of as right or wrong, good or bad, normal or not normal, important or not important, worth fighting for and not worth fighting for, worth saying and doing and not worth saying and doing, and so on. Our values define who we are by shaping what we will and won't do. If you value people, you won't harm them. If you value protecting nature, you won't carelessly pollute it. If you value honesty, you won't deceive people. Your values provide, in essence, a "blueprint" for your behavior, a map to follow in the way you live your life. Your values can give your life meaning. Likewise, a lack of meaningful values can define you as reckless, uncaring, and a walking hazard to others.

In relation to depression, so often people are unclear about themselves and are uncertain as to how they feel, what they value, or how to act. Without a clear code to live by, you can simply be led by whatever impulse pops up in the moment and then may end up doing things that range from foolish to destructive. How can you develop self-respect or earn the respect of others, which is the glue of healthy relationships, if you just lurch from impulse to impulse?

The process called "values clarification" involves identifying your values and developing them into a purposeful "code to live by," a deliberate and consistent way of dealing with the various things that go on in your life. Having a structure in place—a set of meaningful standards you set for yourself—gives you the chance to behave in ways that allow you to develop and maintain a healthy respect for yourself. It's how good self-esteem gets built, and it's how others come to trust you as reliable and consistent. You can start defining your values with statements such as, "When I'm angry, I will say or do this but I won't say or do that." or, "When I'm stressed out, I'll do this but I won't do that." What leads to self-recriminations and poor self-esteem so often is disappointing yourself when you act in a way that is contrary to what you value.

Some people adopt the code of "Christian," some adopt the code of "United States Marine," and some adopt the code of "Practice random acts of kindness." The important thing is to know and understand your core values and live a life that reflects them well. To help you determine your code to live by, write down some statements, like the ones above and fill in the actual statements. For example, "When I'm angry, I'll let a person know I'm feeling anger and may even need to leave a room to cool down, but I won't say something mean that can't be taken back once it's spoken."

#27 Take Sensible Action to Do and *Be* Better Sooner Rather Than Later

How long should you stew about some situation that really bothers you? How long should you endure suffering? At what point should you say, "Enough!" and try to do something to improve things?

I'm speaking in general terms, of course, since I'm not addressing any specific person or situation here. In general, the goal is to curtail stewing and minimize suffering at the soonest possible moment. After all, there's no great sense of accomplishment to be gained from suffering needlessly.

The importance of taking sensible action cannot be overstated. Action is *crucial* to overcoming depression. Why, then, would people just endure stewing and suffering instead of doing something to help themselves get better? There at least these three possibilities:

1. The person doesn't recognize the stress and bad feelings building and likely won't until they reach an almost-crisis proportion. Too many people don't recognize the smaller signs of something needing attention and therefore don't react until the problems have gotten *huge*. For example, someone may miss being stressed until he/she has a heart attack or migraine; someone doesn't know he/she is full until he/she is uncomfortably stuffed; and someone doesn't know he/she is tired until he/she passes out from exhaustion. One would have to learn to recognize bad feelings in milder forms *before* they blossom into full-blown depression.

2. The person is caught up in the erroneous belief that no amount of effort will change anything, which gives rise to the help-

lessness so often found in depression sufferers. This prevents them from seeking help, assuring the depression will continue on and likely get worse over time.

3. The person knows he or she needs to do *something*, but has no idea what exactly that would be. So, unless he or she takes some action to consult someone with knowledge and experience in working with people who suffer depression (e.g., a psychotherapist or a life coach) who can help identify what steps to take and in what order, that person can stay stuck simply because he/she lacks an action plan.

The longer you stew, the longer you suffer, and the more time depression has to take root in your life. Then, as it grows, it contaminates more and more of your life. The price for waiting is paid in feeling bad about yourself, damaged relationships, poor decisions that make things worse, and on and on. Please, don't wait to take action in your own behalf. As far as I know, you only go around once, and every day counts.

#28 Learn to Better Recognize Cause and Effect in Order to Eventually Make Better Predictions

How good are your predictions about your own behavior or the behavior of others? Are you often surprised by things happening, often unpleasant, that you never saw coming? It's hard to "get out of the way" if you can't see it coming at you.

People say things such as, "The future can't be predicted," or, "Life is what happens to you when you had other plans." While it's true that not everything can be predicted, or perhaps even most things, there is a great deal that *can* be predicted. You can predict that if you smoke, you're likely to have serious health problems. You can predict that if you treat people dishonestly or with hostility, you will regularly alienate people. Too often, though, people just don't see the connection between the things they do and the consequences they generate. For example, they'll complain their significant other was "too needy" and never realize they helped make them that way by *overdoing things for them*, which actively discouraged their greater independence.

Cause-and-effect thinking means you can clearly see the relationship between actions and consequences. Sometimes it's easy to see cause and effect, like flipping a light switch and seeing the light go on. Sometimes the cause isn't so clear, as in depression itself where there can be many contributing factors clouding your vision. But more often than you might realize, there are trends in behavior that make people more predictable in terms of the actions they take. For example, recognizing your tendency to blame yourself when someone hurts you, as if you "deserved it," directly leads to the effect of letting others "off the hook" for their bad behavior. It should be no surprise, then, when they behave badly and still find a way to blame *you*.

Cause-and-effect thinking applies to knowing your own vulnerabilities, meaning, the triggers that are unique to your own experience of depression. If you understand that the "cause" is *this* kind of interaction (i.e., someone laying a "guilt trip" on you or someone threatening to leave you) and the "effect" is to feel worthless and helpless, then you can take direct and active steps to learn to better manage those kinds of interactions.

When you can skillfully read people and situations—observing the patterns in them that eventually influence what happens—you will be able to see things coming at you more often and you will have time to take steps to prevent getting run over. You can't predict everything, of course, but you can predict more than you might realize.

#29 You Will Have to Live With the Choices You Make, So It's Important to Make Good Ones

One of the unfortunate consequences of the notion of "depression as a disease" is the associated belief that you "catch it" somehow. As you now know, depression can come about for *many* reasons and is the product of many different personal vulnerabilities or risk factors. One of the most common pathways into depression may be found in the quality of your decision-making.

There is plenty of evidence to show that depression doesn't usually "just happen" to some unfortunate person. Rather, there is a process known as "stress generation," and its primary characteristic is the way in which decisions are made that can either cause depression or make depression worse. To put it plainly, instead of thinking the depressed person is a passive and unfortunate victim of depression, the scientific evidence says something else: the person *might* be contributing to his or her own misery by making bad decisions that make the depression worse. In such instances, the decisions are usually made unintentionally, of course, but are made nonetheless.

Your spouse says, "Honey, you're struggling emotionally. Why don't you get some help?" Your reply is, "Leave me alone!" *Bad decision.* Your doctor says your symptoms suggest depression and you should follow up with the prescription for antidepressants and the recommendation for therapy. You throw out the prescription on your way out of the office and never make an appointment for therapy. *Bad decision.* Your friend tells you you're not handling something very well. You tell him or her to "mind your own business." *Bad decision.*

The internal orientation, the tendency to use your (depressed) feelings as the indicator of what to do, means you are likely to make decisions based on depression. The likelihood, therefore, is to make decisions that are contaminated by your mood that end up being poor decisions. It would be especially wise and helpful in terms of prevention to double-check the merits of your decision-making process and the decision itself, especially for bigger decisions that can have a significant impact on your life and the lives of those who depend on you to one extent or another. In fact, if you are aware that you're in a particularly depressed state, making any important decision should be avoided until you can do a reality check. The value of another opinion can't be overstated. It doesn't mean you have to follow someone else's viewpoint necessarily, but it can open up a dialogue that makes your decision-making process more likely to be an effective one.

#30 To Feel Good, You Need to Do the Things That Make You Feel Good

When you're depressed, your desire to do much of anything slowly dwindles away. Eventually, you only do what you have to do and stop doing the things that you enjoy. In fact, you may have even forgotten what you enjoy doing. This is what mental health professionals call "anhedonia," the loss of pleasure, that is often associated with depression. When you stop taking pleasure in activities that you normally enjoy, it means you've probably already been too depressed for too long.

It's easy to work against yourself. Your friend calls you and says, "Hey, let's go to a movie." You say, "Nah, I'm too depressed." Your partner says, "Come on, let's go take a walk." You say, "Nah, I don't feel like it." Your kid says, 'C'mon, let's play." You say, "Nah, I'm not in the mood." Little by little, as you build your life around your depressed feelings, your world gets smaller and smaller until all you can see is depression. Your mood becomes top-heavy, and your quality of life collapses under its weight.

True story: When I was a university student, I was terribly overloaded with academic courses, research, a full-time job, family commitments, and routine chores needing to be done. I slept too little, didn't socialize, and, to make a long story short, I was stressed, unhappy, and just plain grim. At a very infrequent social event I managed to attend, I met a guy wearing a T-shirt that had two cartoon stick figures sitting on a see-saw and the phrase printed underneath read, "It's OK to play." He asked me what I did, and I asked him what he did. He said, "I'm a recreational therapist." I had never heard of this before, so he explained, "I teach people to play." I dismissively thought, "*Yeah*, that's *useful*." Some days later, I came to the realization that I needed his help!

He asked me to make a list of at least twenty-five things I really enjoyed doing and bring it to him. That was easy since there were many things I enjoyed. Then he asked me, "When was the last time you did any of these?" There wasn't one thing on my list I had done in the last six months, and most I hadn't done in over a year!

He made the obvious point: "How are you supposed to feel good if you don't *regularly* do the things that make you feel good?" Now, I pose the same question to *you*. Unless you deliberately and regularly *make the time* to do things that are fun, playful, and light, it's way too easy to focus only on the inevitable burdens that can make life, well, *depressing*.

#31 There Is No One So Powerful as Someone on a Mission

If you stop and think about people you have known who were powerful people, not because of their job title or status, but just because of the way they are, they are people who are driven to achieve some goal, whatever that goal might be. For some, it's seeing their children grow up well and become successful. For others, it's writing a book, creating a lovely garden, or a work of art. For others, it's getting a college degree, finding a cure for cancer, or serving their community. The goal itself doesn't matter nearly as much as the intense drive the person feels toward accomplishing the goal.

If you think about it, the times in *your* life when you have been the most powerful have been the times when you had a goal—a *mission*, really—that was so compelling to you that you were unstoppable. It's one of the debilitating side effects of depression that nothing much seems worth the effort, especially when there's the negative expectation that the effort will just be wasted because "it'll never happen." The easiest way to create apathy is to ask, "Why bother?" At the extreme, one could say, "We're all going to die one day, so what's the point of even trying?" That attitude makes everything equally trivial and devoid of value. It's a massive case of "sour grapes"—a saying derived from the old Aesop's fable about the fox that tried hard but failed to reach a desirable bunch of grapes. After great and exhausting effort, the fox finally gave up and declared, "They were probably sour anyways." We tend to put down what we can't have, and we quickly give up when we think effort is doomed.

If you're reading this book, it's because you don't want depression to influence the course of your life. As your insights grow about how you de-motivate yourself and give up on your goals, perhaps by making them seem unattainable or making it seem as if the effort involved is so great as to be impossible, then you might learn to establish new goals for yourself in each area of your life. What do you want for yourself in terms of career, health, income, social life, recreation, service to others, creativity, intimacy, etc.? Your life is made up of these and many other components as well, so to spend some time exploring what you want in each area of your life can help you discover, or perhaps *re*-discover, what provides you with a life direction and the motivation to keep moving in that direction even when you encounter challenges along the way. As Yogi Berra, the legendary baseball player famous for mangling his sentences said, "You got to be careful if you don't know where you're going because you might not get there."

There is no one so powerful as someone on a mission. That someone can be *you.*

#32 A Goal Without Steps Is Just a Wish

I wish I had a dollar for every client who came in, sat down, and said, "All I want is to be happy. Is that too much to ask?" Or, those who said, "All I want is a good relationship. Isn't that okay?" Could a request be any more global or undefined than these? When I ask for greater definition, "What do you think it takes to have a good relationship?" the person replies with an equally global answer, "Chemistry."

I have emphasized the importance of having goals, but they must be well-defined goals that make effort more likely to succeed. Notice I didn't say "guaranteed" to succeed, only *more likely* to succeed. There are few guarantees in life. No one who plants a garden, directs a movie, has a child, applies for a job, or takes a course is guaranteed success. But, you can't pass the class if you don't first sign up for it, nor can your garden grow without first planting the seeds, nor can you get the job if you don't first apply for it.

In previously discussing the "global cognitive style" (#20: Learn to Think Critically and in Greater Detail), I made the point that it's most improbable to solve specific problems with over-general thinking. Specific problems generally require specific solutions. Similarly, you can't expect to reach specific goals with just a general approach. It requires defining the goal in very specific terms and even more than that, defining the specific steps that will be necessary to take to reach that goal.

When someone tells me, "I just want to be happy," I'll ask them to do an important exercise you may want to do, too. I call it "A Flow of Steps," and it asks the person to create a flow chart—a sequence of detailed steps to take—to do something pretty basic, such as taking a shower. "Taking a shower" is a global term; you don't "take a shower," you follow *a series of steps* that result in you being clean. The task I give the client is to create a sequence that *anyone* can follow that will assure their success in the endeavor. Some people generate as few as three steps ("get wet, lather up, rinse off") while others generate over fifty detailed steps and provide an easily duplicated sequence that fulfills the task of assuring someone else's success in taking a shower. Then, I'll ask the person to do the same kind of flow chart for "how to be happy." Almost instantly they realize it's not because they're undeserving of happiness or are just unlucky. They discover they don't know how—they don't have any idea what steps to follow or they have some steps and get stuck along the way. Then they become more open to learning what steps to follow to get where they want to go.

By having well-defined steps to follow, even including the steps to follow when it's unclear what steps to follow, it helps breaks a very large goal into smaller pieces that can be accomplished. Each step in the right direction provides feedback, so there is encouragement along the way. Then, when times get tough, there's a specific point to stop and make adjustments or corrections without having to feel as if "everything" went wrong and that you should just give up trying.

It will help you much more to have a *tight plan* for succeeding than just making a wish.

Part 3:
Key People Skills Necessary to Manage Depression

#33 Isolation Can Feed Irrationality

There are many different reasons why having warm, supportive relationships in your life can be critically important to your overall well-being. It is literally true that the human brain is "wired" to be social and that relationships affect mental functioning in a variety of powerful ways. Do *you* have close, positive relationships with others?

Currently, loneliness is on the rise. More people are living alone than ever before, more people report being lonely too much of the time, and too many people admit they don't have anyone in which they can confide. So, to get their social needs met, some will join online chatrooms and fool themselves into thinking these are real relationships (they're not). No chatroom acquaintance can take you to the doctor or pick you up from your dental appointment, or take some groceries to your mom when you're out of town. Others just withdraw completely, isolating themselves from others as a way of life.

Far more important than having friends to help with your errands is the fact that when you don't have anyone to confide in, someone whose opinions you respect, you end up alone with your thoughts. And what happens if those thoughts are distorted or simply wrong? By having someone to talk to on a deeper, more honest and personal level, your friend can challenge your thinking in helpful ways. You don't realize the ways you twist information, distort the facts, ignore inconvenient bits of information, and do what *all* of us naturally do in creating beliefs that are too easily believed if we don't open them up to examination, the process of "reality-testing" (as discussed in #18: Do Not Believe Yourself: Reality Test).

It takes time to develop good relationships, especially if you've been socially isolative for a while or don't have the best of social skills for engaging well with people. The fact that it may not be easy for you, however, doesn't mean it isn't worth doing. It's so important to bring others into your life who can both support and challenge you and, likewise, for you to be that important person for others. Yours can be the opinion that makes a difference for someone else just as readily as his or her opinion can make a difference for you. You don't always have to agree with people, of course, nor do they always have to agree with you, but it can make your life much smoother and better when you have others to confide in who can help you when your thinking drifts off the path. It's too easy to go off in hurtful directions in your perceptions when you don't seek out reality checks.

In addition to these reasons for connecting to others, being with people also helps you "get out of yourself" for a while. When you're caught up in depression, you're typically self-absorbed in your own bad feelings. Having other people around interrupts that, even if only for a short time, and it allows you to focus on and experience something other than just your bad mood. (That assumes, of course, that you make an effort to be at least somewhat pleasant for others to be around.) It can also remind you that you can deliberately change the way you feel, even if just temporarily, and thus have first-hand experience at creating conditions for feeling better.

I am not suggesting you become a social butterfly. Rather, I am encouraging you to understand the value of what other people can bring to your life and how they can help in overcoming your depression, even when you think the last thing you want to do right now is be with other people.

#34 Your Mood Affects How You Judge/ Perceive Others

In the same way depression can affect your memory, ability to solve problems, and other cognitive processes (as discussed in #15: Your Mood Affects Your Memory and How You Recall Your Personal History), depression also acts as a filter for making social judgments. Your mood can easily lead you to make negative and even unfair judgments about other people.

Depression can rob you of your sense of humor. When you're in a good mood, things are funny. When you're in a *really* good mood, things are *really* funny. When you're in a *great* mood, earwax is funny! But, when you're in a bad mood, humor has "left the building" and anyone who cracks jokes is judged as silly, annoying, or worse.

Consider these simple examples of the differences in social judgments based on mood:

- When you're in a good mood, sarcasm is funny. When you're in a bad mood, it's mean.
- When you're in a good mood, the person is thrifty. When you're in a bad mood, he or she is cheap.
- When you're in a good mood, he or she is adventurous. When you're in a bad mood, he or she is reckless.
- When you're in a good mood, you think your child is wonderfully energetic. When you're in a bad mood, you think, "Ritalin!"

It's important to have insight about your moods and judgments. Nowhere is this issue more important than when a depressed person is considering separating or divorcing. When you are depressed, it is natural to look for "the reason," and the easiest thing to do may be to blame your partner or spouse for your depression. There may even be some truth to the perception that this person is damaging to be around. But how do you know whether it's depression leading you to unfairly blame that person for your unhappiness, or whether you're right to believe that in order to move forward with your life you need to leave that person behind?

Until you filter the depression out of the decision-making process, it would be too easy to make a potentially very costly life error. *Before* you decide to divorce and *especially* if you have kids, it would be wise to see a professional who can help you sort out what's actually a result of your partner and what's a result of your mood in this circumstance. *This is an opportunity to prevent regret.* You don't want to unnecessarily and permanently break up a relationship over a temporary depression.

This is true not only for relationship decisions but for all important decisions: keep or quit a job, make a large purchase or sell a large asset, engage in or pass up a business deal, choose to have a child, *whatever*. These are not decisions to be made through the filter of depressed mood. If such important decisions need to be made, however, then it is critical that you seek outside or professional guidance to help you assess all factors to make the clearest decision possible without the depression contaminating your decision.

#35 Skip the Depression Stigma and Learn From Other People's Experience: There Is No Need to Re-Invent the Quality-Of-Life Wheel

Depressed people too often miss the chance to get the help they need because they fear other people's negative judgments or even their own negative judgments, the so-called "stigma of depression" that makes directly facing depression undesirable. They think they "should be stronger" and seeking help for depression is an "admission of weakness." People have also been told that depression is an illness or disease, yet they don't *feel* "diseased" or "sick." Rather, they feel stressed, unhappy, overwhelmed, tired, under-appreciated, harangued, harassed, and lots more, but they don't *feel* "mentally ill."

I think the "depression as mental illness" perspective was meant to help people feel blameless so they'd be less ashamed and self-condemning about their depression. Being told, as many people are, that they are no more responsible for their depression than epileptics are for their seizures is meant to reduce the stigma so they would then be more likely to get help. It didn't work out that way, however. Most depressed people *don't* seek help, instead just suffering in silence and trying to cope alone day to day. That's such a shame, because good help can literally turn your life around, but you'd have to see past the label "depression" and better understand what influences your mood and outlook. *You're more than a diagnostic label.*

Frankly, I don't really care very much about the label "depression." I'm much more interested in the *quality of life* you are experiencing, what you feel your life is about, and whether it's proving to be a satisfying and worthwhile life to you. Given how "soft" or imprecise the diagnosis of depression is, I'd much prefer we focus on how you can improve your quality of life. One of the best tools for doing so is to be observant of others, especially others who face similar challenges to you but who seem to manage them more effectively than you do. *You can learn from them.* Instead of wondering why you're unhappy and they're not, use your curiosity to find out! Curiosity is one of the best resources for stimulating learning and using what you learn to improve your quality of life.

By isolating yourself, focusing on just getting by, struggling with your personal feelings and life challenges, other people are typically viewed as part of the problem rather than part of the solution. If you are a good observer, though, by definition *externally oriented* in situations involving other people, you'll notice that there are people all around you all the time who are good at doing something, *whatever* it might be. There are people who are good at keeping their desk clean, returning email in a timely way, making people comfortable in their homes, setting limits with their demanding kids, making others feel appreciated, and so on.

The key question for you to consider when you see someone who is good at something is, "*How* does he or she do that?" What can you learn about the steps people follow to do the things they do well? This is the precise challenge I set for myself in learning to be a clinician providing treatment to depression sufferers. What could I learn from people who face terrible adversities but do *not* become depressed? How do effective people make key life decisions? How do happy couples build satisfying relationships? What do such people actually *do*?

There are so many life lessons to be found in just watching and learning from people who are good at what they do. That requires getting out of yourself long enough to notice people around you who are effective, and even taking the risk of asking them questions directly about their skills if the situation is appropriate. There are many people who have overcome depression and they are worth interviewing. In fact, that's been one very important way I've learned so much about getting over depression: asking people how they handled *this* or what they learned that helped them with *that*. I've been so impressed with people who were great at explaining how they do what they do, and the many life strategies I've learned from such people have proven invaluable.

This is another good reason to also consider talking to a professional who knows and can teach you effective life strategies. It's not a stigma of depression you need to overcome. Instead, it's about *building up your curiosity* as to what you can learn from others that can help you move your life forward in satisfying ways. You really don't have to struggle on your own to reinvent the "feel good" quality-of-life wheel.

#36 Beware of the Potentially Negative Effects Technology Has on Depression: Be Smarter Than Your Smartphone!

Most of us have smartphones. Surveys show that most of us can't go for more than a few hours without checking our smartphones for email and texts. There is no going back to how things were before technology became so heavily integrated into our lives, so it's wasted breath to talk about "the good old days" when people actually talked to each other directly and looked at each other at dinner instead of their phones. Even though technology has become so deeply integrated into our lives, it isn't without mood consequences as well as changes in social behavior and learning styles (as discussed in #20: Learn to Think Critically and in Greater Detail).

What are the effects of technology on perception and mood? So many of the changes in our lives are new and still unfolding that it's hard to be precise. But these techno-gadgets indulge people in a number of ways, such as the instant availability of people and information, the immediacy of getting responses from friends, the ever-present entertainment of games and shows to occupy your every quiet moment, and the sheer number of people you can reach with a click of a button. With immediacy, convenience, and self-indulgence as the technology's addictive qualities, consider all that is human that is marginalized. There's a price to pay when your smartphone is smarter than you, when *it owns you* instead of the other way around.

More than one study has linked how much time you spend in front of a computer screen with how bad you are likely to feel. It's not the technology itself that may be a problem for someone. It's what the technology encourages—and discourages—in thinking and behaving that's the potential problem. You can't learn *social skills*, such as carrying on a good conversation or reading people's facial expressions as they speak when all you're doing is texting or emailing. You can't develop *frustration tolerance* when you want answers right now. You can't develop *critical thinking skills* when you just absorb whatever the screen tells you is true even when it isn't. You can't build a *real relationship* typing messages back and forth in a chatroom.

There's another technology-based issue of great concern, namely the relationship between bullying, technology, and depression. Teens today are especially heavily influenced by online postings about them that can be unbelievably mean. While parents still think that sex and drugs are the big issues for their teens, the teens themselves say in surveys that they're more concerned about bullying and their mental health. Technology means you can bully people anonymously and post the most embarrassing and even degrading stories and images for the whole world to see. The bullying no longer ends at the end of the school day as it used to when you finally got to go to the relative safety of home. Now it's about slamming people twenty-four hours a day in the view of *everybody* starting in grade school and continuing on into college and even beyond into the work environment. Mental health professionals are still trying to figure out what to do about this alarming phenomenon that is contributing so greatly to teen depression that predictably can become a basis for adult depression, too. Add to that the sexting (sending nude pictures of yourself to a partner you may think are private but aren't) and the revenge postings of embarrassing pictures to get back at someone who has broken up with you. The Internet is then serving as a weapon that can keep hurting you forever since those posts will always be there for anyone diligent enough to look for them. Furthermore, the Internet provides yet another pathway into depression when people go on Facebook and get fooled into thinking everyone else's life is going great while theirs is limping along.

The technology isn't going away and these various issues will need to be worked out as a new code of conduct emerges. But it makes it even more important to your mental health to have days, or at least large sections of days, that are "unplugged," where technology is set aside in favor of *human pursuits* such as conversations, time spent in nature, meditation, self-exploration, creative expression, and other paths to personal growth. Once you are clear that technology skews your perceptions and thinking processes in ways that are sometimes unhelpful and even depressing, it may be easier for you to deliberately create chunks of time spent reminding yourself what it means to be a fully alive human being.

#37 Your Depression Inevitably Affects Others: Protect Them With Sensitive Management Strategies

Depression too often gets treated as if it is just one person's problem. In fact, on average, *at least* three other people are negatively affected by a depressed person's mood and behavior. If you're depressed, are you aware of who else in *your* life you may be affecting in undesirable ways? If you've never really thought about it before, it can be disturbing to realize that whatever is going on with you can be hurting others, especially those closest to you. It's not intentional meanness. It's a reflection of feeling bad. But it still needs to be contained with good personal boundaries.

Working with couples and families where at least one adult partner is dealing with depression, I have encountered the situation far too many times where the depressed person is irritable, impatient, and even hostile much of the time. Depression can and regularly does do that to people. The other partner and kids will confess, if you make it safe for them to do so, that they are nearly always "walking on eggshells" around the depressed person. That means they live with the constant anxiety that they will either do something to set the person off or just be his or her "whipping post" if they happen to be around when something bothersome happens. It poisons the family atmosphere.

When I hear from the kids or the partner what kinds of things the depressed person is saying that are so hurtful and mean, I *have to* intervene. I have to say something like, "I'm *really* sorry you're depressed, but that doesn't give you the right to say these kinds of nasty things to your family. Always remember, your depression is very likely to go away and soon. But your family members will be hearing the echoes in their minds of what you said for *years*." It is an immediate goal to learn to contain and protect others from your negativity. It helps them, but it also helps you. You'll like yourself better and feel more in control when you learn enough impulse control to think twice (or even three times) before you say something potentially hurtful. That skill will also help you long after the depression has lifted, because it's just the kind of decency you find in healthy relationships where partners protect rather than abuse each other.

If you need to vent, see a therapist. If you're frustrated and angry, see a therapist. If you're hurting others and want to protect them, see a therapist. It is just irresponsible to wait and wait and hope the depression goes away while you're harming your most important relationships. Your problems should not contaminate other people's lives.

#38 If You Are Depressed, Your Kids Are at Risk for Depression Too: Help Prevent Your Children From Getting That Particular Inheritance From You

The child of a depressed parent is at least three times more likely to develop depression than a child without a depressed parent. Just having a depressed parent is a very large risk factor for children's depression. Now that we know it's *not* because of a "depression gene," it points to the way depressed parents interact with their kids, especially the way they model interpreting and reacting to life experiences.

Every time your child asks "why" about something, your answer inevitably teaches that child something about how to think (or not), how to react, what to prioritize and value, and much more. Every time you say things impulsively you have to apologize for later (if you even have the grace to apologize, which many people don't), every time you avoid a situation or say you don't want to talk about it, each time you slam doors and make threats or get drunk when you're upset, you're teaching your child the kinds of things that will lead them closer to their own depression. *You can't teach kids what you don't know.*

The more aware you become of how your experience of depression can warp your interactions with all others, but especially vulnerable children, the more care you can take to choose your words and actions wisely, with insight and foresight. Recognizing at all times that you are your child's role model for how someone should think and act, you have to be responsible for your position as the parent at all times, not just when you feel like it or when it's convenient. That doesn't mean you'll never make mistakes, but they'll be fewer and less terribly costly ones.

Besides providing a safe and stable home environment, teaching your child how to be a *critical thinker* and how to *interact well* with others are very likely the two most important things you can do to prevent them from developing depression. When depression prevention programs have been created and implemented in schools that teach these things, the results have been wonderful.

#39 Be Selective About Whom You Open Up to About Your Problems in General and Your Depression in Particular

When you're depressed and almost constantly focused on how bad you're feeling, you could easily walk around telling anyone and everyone how much you're suffering if you don't have some good filters in place. To do so is unwise.

You probably spend a great deal of time with your coworkers, and it might seem the easiest and most natural thing to do to confide in them about your depression. Should you? And what about your supervisor, manager, or boss? Should you tell him or her about your depression? What too many people don't realize is there might be a hefty price to pay for revealing your depression to the wrong people. Some people just don't understand depression and only carry ideas based on myths that can subject you to inappropriate prejudices.

Could the term "depression" get placed in your work file and become an issue when it comes time for a promotion or even just an annual performance review? Could the label "depressive" jeopardize your career in some way even though you have overcome it and are doing well? Could others see you as either less capable or more fragile and change in undesirable ways how they treat and work with you? Could it jeopardize your ability to get health insurance or result in higher premiums because of the way depression is viewed?

These are tough questions and they represent just some of the ways people can misunderstand and react inappropriately to the depression label. If your depression is interfering with your work and might jeopardize your career, get professional help right away. You don't want to cause permanent damage to your career because of a temporary depression.

Your family members are the people you are closest to and it seems the most natural thing to openly share with them whatever is going on with you. But, once again, you have to be careful. Sharing with your spouse or partner is important and as your (presumably) primary intimate relationship, being open and honest is important. But that's only if the relationship is a warm, supportive one. Unfortunately, there are some people who use open and honest disclosures as ammunition against you the next time you get in an argument. It comes back at you and it is hurtful. The general idea is to know whether the relationship, with *whomever* it might be, can support your disclosure with compassion and respect.

This point is especially true with your kids. Should you tell them what's going on with you? With younger kids, they may well know something is wrong but not know how to articulate it much less understand it. If you know your depression is affecting them, you really should acknowledge this in some way. But you don't need to use the label "depression" or call it an illness that can scare kids or cause them to fear that you won't be a reliable parent they can count on to fully be there for them when they need you. Kids need the assurance that Mom and Dad are stable and reliable. So, you can share in a very general way that you "haven't been feeling so well lately" if you detect their concern and give them the assurances they need that you love them and you'll be okay. Do your best to protect them from your mood issues and do what you can to address depression sooner rather than later.

Be alert to the effects your depression has on others. Some people are observant and can see that you seem to be more moody lately, but others see very little beyond themselves, so don't assume everyone can tell you're depressed. Some may even directly ask you what's going on, and you should be prepared with an answer you've already thought out well in advance. Decide whom you can tell what to and in how much detail so you're not caught off guard and end up disclosing things you may regret later.

If your depression is placing you in uncomfortable positions with other people and may jeopardize your job or primary relationships, getting through the depressive episode as soon as possible is important. This is another good reason *not to delay* getting help from a good psychotherapist. What can make depression so devastating for people is all the career and family wreckage left behind because they didn't ask for help until it had already gotten way out of hand.

You can't confide in everyone or just anyone. It has to be someone safe and professional who can actually help you. For everyone else, I'd suggest you conservatively keep your disclosures on a "need to know" basis.

#40 People Can Be More—or Less—Than They Seem: Learn to Assess Them Realistically

One of the most depressing circumstances is when you get emotionally attached to someone who becomes a source of distress instead of a source of comfort. When a relationship is going great, it can be exhilarating. But when a relationship is going badly, it can be excruciating. Bringing the right people into your life is critically, vitally important.

We all live in a world filled with other people, and there is no escaping their presence or their influence, but we don't deal with everyone all at once. We move from one interaction to another, and even in large social situations we typically are still speaking with others on a one-to-one basis. When you first meet and are starting to get to know someone, what do you tend to notice about that person? What kind of assessment process, if any, do you go through to try to get a sense of who this person is?

The internal orientation of depression (discussed in #18: "Don't Believe Yourself: Reality Test,") often precludes making much of an assessment of others. You can get so focused on yourself ("Do I look okay? Am I making enough eye contact? What should I say next? I wonder if he or she is noticing my pimple.") that you pay too little attention to the other person, missing potentially important information about him or her. Or, you can incorrectly and naively assume that other people are just like you. They're *not*. By learning to be more *externally* oriented—more observant about the nature of the person you're interacting with—you can make better decisions about *whether* to have some kind of relationship (business, social, romantic) and if so to what extent.

People are typically quite revealing. Most people like to talk about themselves and more often than not tell you more than you really want to know. Others are more guarded and reveal little about themselves, which in itself can reveal a lot about them. Likewise, you are revealing things about yourself with the comments you make, the information you share, the jokes you tell, the things you react to that others say, and so on. So, it's really not a question of *whether* people will reveal things about themselves; it's a matter of whether you recognize what they're saying with their words and also what they're saying "between the lines." If you "read" someone incorrectly, you are much more likely to be caught off-guard and even get hurt by things they do that you didn't anticipate.

Sometimes people can and do behave in surprisingly inconsistent ways. Most of the time, though, people act in predictable ways that are consistent with their values and temperament. Thus, we really can learn to rely on someone to do *this* and trust him or her not to do *that*. That's why learning to assess people realistically is such an important skill to develop. If you're going to be in a relationship with someone, meaning, an ongoing association (with a coworker, supervisor, neighbor, friend, business acquaintance, group member), then it will help to better understand who this person is and what is reasonable to expect from him or her.

What are the things you might make a point of noticing? I'd suggest it's vitally important to know where this person places the responsibility for his or her actions. Relationships are challenging enough without having to deal with people who do questionable things and then place the blame elsewhere for their actions. Along the same line of responsibility, it is critically important for someone to do the things he or she has the responsibility to do. For example, if you have to chase someone around to have a meaningful talk because he or she doesn't "feel like it," this should tell you that the person won't be there when something difficult needs to be addressed. Not much else matters if the person doesn't handle responsibilities well.

There are many other things to pay attention to as well. These include the person's values (what he or she defines as important, often learnable to an extent from observing where he or she spends his or her time and money), degree of self-awareness, ability to identify and articulate feelings and other internal experiences, ability to respectfully accept differences in your viewpoints and interests, ability to contain anger and other strong emotions, ability to put the relationship ahead of personal gain at your expense, and more.

It takes a deliberate and perceptive person to learn to assess others realistically. When the relationship is unavoidable, such as with others on the job or with family members, you can learn to modify how much and what type of contact you have with them based on your judgment. Similarly, with people you date or socialize with, you can gauge how far to let things go based on what you learn about them. The biggest payoff for developing these skills is when you *don't* have to deal with other people's frequent dramas. Other people can be a source of great comfort or serious pain. *Choose wisely whom you bring into your life.*

#41 People Will Take Everything You Have If You Let Them: Protect Yourself

Sometimes the pathway into depression is to give and give to someone who is willing to take and take. Whatever you have, somebody wants it. Whether it's your money, your time, your body, your advice, your support, your expertise, your compliance, your connections, *whatever* you have, somebody wants it. How do you protect yourself from those who would drain you of whatever you have and give back little or nothing?

To protect yourself from others willing to exploit you, you would need to first develop and maintain great clarity about your boundaries. Boundaries define you in terms of what you are and are not willing to say or do, what you will and won't allow others to say and do to you, and what you will defend when others push you to get what they want. Boundaries translate into highly practical patterns of interaction, such as whether you'll let your kid move back home again or lend your lazy cousin even more money, or have sex with someone you don't even like that much just to stop the whining.

The need for self-awareness in order to build boundaries is obvious. The skills needed next are recognizing what someone wants from you, maybe even before he or she does, and what manipulative tactics he or she will use to go after what he or she wants.

Do you know when you are being manipulated? There are lots of different tactics people use to get what they want:

- Guilt ("If you leave me I'll kill myself.")
- Fear and intimidation ("Don't push me or I swear I'll make your life miserable.")

- Flattery ("But you're the only person who can possibly do this.")
- Greed ("If you give me the money, I promise I'll pay you back twice as much.")
- Abandonment ("I can't be with you if you're not going to do it my way.")
- Cold shoulder ("Don't talk to me, don't even look at me.")
- Sympathy ("But if you don't do it for me, I'll be miserable.")

All of these ploys are effective ways to get others to do what you want. The price is exacted in how bad such ploys make you or others feel, and that's why they are abusive. When you know what others want, you're in the driver's seat. You get to decide whether to give them what they want, or not, and you may well decide just on the basis of whether they ask cleanly and respectfully or whether they are willing to hurt you to get what they want. (It also helps if you have the integrity not to do that kind of thing to others.)

The next skill in this process is to manage conflict well if it arises when you say "no" to someone. "Conflict avoidance" is the term psychologists use to describe the tendency to simply give in to someone's demands just to avoid the ensuing hassle they create when they don't like your "no" answer. Conflict avoidance is the most common reason why people don't assert themselves. Nobody really likes conflict, but we come to accept it as inevitable if we're going to protect ourselves from when others' demands or behaviors "cross the line" we've set for ourselves.

The people in your life who are generally the most troublesome are the ones you know well, your family and friends. They've learned which of your "buttons to push." Learning to quickly recognize what they want *this* time, and how they're going after it *again*, you can anticipate what the interaction is going to be like and *be ready for it*. Instead of getting caught off-guard as if you didn't know it was coming sooner or later, you can have a few really clever boundary defining responses ready to go so that you don't cave in and then beat yourself up for having done so.

#42 Dare to Be Superficial—*Sometimes*

One of the mistakes that people typically make when they gradually develop depression is when they start to build their life around it. They withdraw from friends and family, stop doing the things they normally enjoy doing, and resist attempts others make to engage them in conversation or activities, thereby virtually guaranteeing the depression will continue. They do this unintentionally, of course, but they still do it.

One of the first casualties of depression is *fun*. Depressed people are not generally known for their sense of humor, and fun seems improbable when you feel bad and, even more than that, seeking fun seems a superficial and even "stupid" way of spending time when life is filled with such serious problems. I've heard from so many depressed people that they just "can't bear the superficiality or happiness of others" when they're depressed. They want people to be as serious and even grim as they are, acknowledging and respecting their suffering. Anything else seems a cruel taunting of their emotional pain.

There will *always* be problems to handle. If you're alive, you face problems. To be so burdened by problems—whether through rumination or unwittingly doing things that make situations worse rather than better—that you can't also see the positive aspects of life is both one-sided and hurtful. It requires a boundary, an ability to set aside the serious and the burdensome to give time to the pleasant and superficial. The grease of human relationships is superficial banter, the simple enjoyment of being able to have fun together *sometimes*. The joy of living is in the fun of activities that aren't particularly deep but just feel good.

To be "deep" in your thinking or relationships is a *potential*, not a *mandate*. If all you can be is superficial, then you are limited. But the reverse is also true, for if all you can be is deep, you are equally limited. Deep has its place at times, but so does superficial. Instead of angrily or impatiently branding people who want to enjoy you or have some fun with you as trite or worse, you would do better to go to the silly movie or the big game with them and recognize this isn't the time or place to get "heavy" in either attitude or conversation. And then, *enjoy yourself.*

This is especially true when managing your family when you're depressed. Make a point of *initiating* fun times and set firm boundaries that prevent you from contaminating the fun time by bringing up problems or criticisms. *It's not the time.* Model the reality that life doesn't have to be perfect in order for it to be darn good. Remind your spouse or partner and kids that you can have personal problems yet still be okay for them to be around. Let your motto at such times be, "*Dare* to be superficial!"

#43 Reduce Your Guilt Load: Get Clear About the Limits of Your Responsibilities

If you look at the diagnostic manuals describing the most common symptom patterns that represent depression, one of the core patterns is "excessive and inappropriate guilt." The first thing that should tell you is that people *can* have guilt that is "excessive," meaning it far exceeds in intensity what is justified by the circumstances. The second thing it should tell you is that guilt *can* be "inappropriate," meaning, the person is feeling guilty for something he or she has no objective reason to feel guilty about. As you've learned, perception can be distorted and not all feelings are accurate.

Here's the heart of the issue: *guilt presupposes responsibility.* You will only feel guilty about the things you believe you are responsible for. This raises the critically important question: *How do you know what you're responsible for?*

The issue of personal responsibility can be a tricky one, to be sure. Most of the time it's crystal clear where the responsibility is for something that has happened. But sometimes it isn't so clear where the responsibility should be placed. For example, consider the fact that depressed people will likely go to a physician for a check-up yet never say to the doctor, "I'm struggling with mood issues." Instead, they'll say, "I'm not sleeping well and I don't have much energy." So, is it the patient's responsibility to tell the doctor, "I'm struggling with mood issues," or is it up to the doctor to figure it out? One could argue either way and make the responsibility issue seem less clear. (Personally, I think it's the patient's responsibility to report accurately what's going on and not expect the doctor to be a mind reader. You might ask, "But, isn't that what professionals get paid to figure out?" Well, yes, but only if they're given enough information to figure it out. The doctor can't really do his or her part until the patient does his or her's first.)

The internal orientation of depression can easily lead you to *reflexively blame yourself* whenever something goes wrong. It reflects a lack of critical thinking, that is, a clear-headed thinking through where the responsibility actually lies in that situation. For people prone to feeling guilty, it's easy for others to blame them for their own bad decisions and avoid personal responsibility ("I wouldn't have been driving drunk if you hadn't criticized me !") because you're willing to assume the blame *for* them. It's not only important that you look at how *you* deal with blame but how *others* around you deal with it, too. If you are willing to accept blame for things for which you're not actually to blame, you end up feeling terrible, and others get off with no consequences for bad behavior. That's bad for *everyone.*

It's important to distinguish between guilt and regret. You can regret something happened, such as your favorite coworker getting fired, but that doesn't make you responsible for it to lead you to feeling guilty that you still have your job. A great life skill is to prevent regret when you can by thinking ahead in your own life to avoid making bad decisions about where responsibility lies. Preventing a feeling of guilt by being clear about what you are and are not responsible for will be a huge help in keeping unnecessary emotional dramas out of your life.

You are responsible for what *you* say and do. You may or may not be responsible for the impact you have on others depending on the circumstances. For example, you lose your home because of your gambling and now your family is out on the street. In that situation, you are responsible for your impact on them. Your girlfriend or boyfriend threatens suicide when you say you want to break up, but you're not responsible since they could make a much better choice to cope than resorting to threatening suicide. You are *not* responsible for the choices others make and the terrible consequences their bad choices often create. You can regret they made that choice, but you are not the one responsible for it.

A huge weight is lifted from your shoulders when you finally get clear about responsibility, guilt, and regret!

Part 4:
Getting Help

#44 Know When You Need Outside Help

I understand the desire to deal with your depression by yourself. In some instances, it may be enough to have the information and the skills I've offered here and in other books to manage on your own. But, throughout this book I have continued to encourage an appreciation of the value of having someone else to talk to for overcoming your own self-limiting thoughts and behaviors. These are some clear signs telling you when you need help if you will take the time to notice and respect them:

- If your depression has led you to develop thoughts of death or suicide (an especially important reason to get help right away);
- If you are depressed and have no idea why or what to do about it;
- If you are suffering distressing symptoms that directly or indirectly interfere with and diminish your quality of life;
- If your depression is negatively affecting people you love, especially your spouse and children.
- If you are getting feedback from others that you need help, and you know it but don't want to face it, the only responsible thing to do is to get help;
- If you have no one close enough to confide in and get feedback from who can challenge and divert you from some or all of your depressed thinking and behavior;
- If you have repeated episodes of depression and have no real understanding as to what your risk factors for relapses are;

- If you are depressed and you have to make a major life decision (such as seeking a divorce, quitting or taking a job, dropping out of school, etc.), and depression may lead you to make a poor decision you'll end up deeply regretting later. Depression is usually a poor frame of mind to be in when making potentially life-changing decisions.
- If you've continued to try to manage it on your own and have not been as successful as you'd like. Early in this book I said that overcoming depression means working smarter, not harder.
- If you've tried therapy or medication and it didn't work – try again. Try a different therapist, a different medication, a different approach, but try again. Do NOT buy into the victim mentality of "Why bother?" In sections forty-five to forty-nine I provide you with additional information that will be helpful in choosing professionals and their services to best help you.

The message I have given you throughout has been this one: You *can* overcome depression but not by chasing your own tail. Your "blind spots" naturally prevent you from seeing yourself clearly, a statement that's true for *all* of us. The value of having someone else to talk to who can fill in the gaps and guide you along a clear path out of depression is immeasurable.

#45 There Are Different Types of Mental Health Professionals

The mental health profession is composed of many different forms of psychotherapy and many different types of psychotherapists. In the broadest sense, a psychotherapist is *anyone* who provides psychological treatment or counseling, regardless of what specific type of therapy he or she practices, or what particular type of degree or license he or she may hold.

Mental health professionals must usually be licensed or certified by a government body in some way in order to practice their profession. The license is granted only when someone has a valid degree from an accredited university, usually (but not always) followed by supervised structured clinical training. Checking on a potential therapist's licensure and qualifications before you begin therapy is a very good idea. This is easy to do in the United States simply by contacting the state licensing board to check on someone's credentials. It may be quite different in other countries. At the very least, you can certainly get some idea of the person's reputation and level of skill by getting a referral from someone you know, such as your own physician or someone who has previously consulted this therapist.

Here is the breakdown of qualified therapists in the United States. These will differ in other countries, but there will likely be close parallels.

A *psychiatrist* is a physician (a medical doctor who has the initials MD after their name) who has an advanced and specialized interest in treating psychological/emotional disorders. Generally, psychiatrists tend to think of psychological problems as a product of faulty brain functioning. Since psychiatrists generally (not always) believe medication and other physical treatments are the best means for helping people, they are not as likely to engage in talk therapies as other types of psychotherapists. However, each psychiatrist is an individual and some do indeed practice talk therapy as part of their treatment approach.

A *clinical psychologist,* also called a doctor because of the doctoral degree earned (usually a PhD or a PsyD), is *not* a medical doctor. A clinical psychologist has an advanced and specialized interest in diagnosing and treating psychological and emotional disorders. Their focus is generally on the psychological and social aspects of a disorder. Psychologists tend to focus on exploring and clarifying the thoughts, feelings, behaviors, and relationships of the person(s) they're treating by using "talk therapies," i.e., talking with and educating the client while focusing on effective problem-solving.

A *marriage and family therapist* (LMFT) has advanced training in the marital and familial aspects of the disorders they treat, while *clinical social workers* often take a larger cultural and community view of the problems they treat. Either of these types of practitioners will have earned master's degrees (MA, MS, or MSW) and will usually have been trained in doing individual psychotherapy as well. This also applies to *licensed professional counselors* (LPCs).

According to research on clinical effectiveness, it is not generally the academic degree that someone holds that determines his or her effectiveness. Rather, it is the ability of the individual therapist to provide a good learning environment that is not only warm and supportive but also goal-oriented. An advanced knowledge of and extensive experience in treating people suffering from depression would obviously be essential for a qualified therapist should you decide to seek professional help.

#46 Choose a Mental Health Professional Wisely

You'll need to do some "shopping" if you are to find a skilled clinician to work with. Therapists are generally well-intentioned people with a sincere desire to help others. But therapy is at least as much art as science, so there is lots of room for individual clinical judgment to influence the course of treatment. To be blunt, some people's judgment simply isn't as good as others. Therefore, you should look for someone who is licensed and therefore accountable, who is well-trained academically (minimum of a master's degree), is positive and empathetic as a person, has extensive clinical experience in treating depressed people, is current with the clinical research, has a good reputation in the community, and who is available for providing treatment to you in a consistent manner.

Do *not* just go to the Internet, phone book, or the local health food restaurant bulletin board to find a therapist. Start by asking family and friends if they've seen a therapist they liked and found effective. Ask your family doctor too (but beware of the "medical brotherhood" that can land you in a psychiatrist/colleague's office and on medication right away in case that isn't what you want). Call the local psychological association (or other local professional associations for marriage, family therapists, or social workers) and get the names of people they'd recommend that specialize in depression.

Once you have some names, call them. Be prepared to do some brief interviewing in order to get someone you feel comfortable with. It's perfectly all right to call and speak to someone for a few minutes (not a half hour or more) about your concerns, and to ask him or her the following key questions:

1. What is your training and clinical experience?
2. Do you have specialized training in treating depression? If so, what is it?
3. How do you generally approach problems such as mine?
4. Are you available for regular appointments?
5. What can I reasonably expect of you if I work with you?
6. What are your fees, and how long are the sessions?
7. Can you accept my health insurance (if you have any)?
8. Do you ever involve family members in treatment? If so, when?

By asking such questions and listening carefully to the responses you get, you will get a sense of who the clinician is as a person and how he or she approaches cases such as yours. If you like what you hear, schedule an appointment and plan to use it as a more careful "shopping" time. If you don't like the person or if you don't develop some confidence that he or she can help, then move on and continue looking for someone else to work with. Be careful not to globally conclude "therapy can't help me" because of a specific therapist (or two) not working out well. It may be difficult to shop when you're depressed, but finding a skilled and knowledgeable therapist is crucial. A good therapist can be a lifesaver in more ways than one.

#47 Establish Reasonable Expectations of Therapy in Order to Get Maximum Benefits

It's essential that your expectations of therapy be realistic in order to avoid disappointment. You should expect a well-trained clinician to gather relevant information about your symptoms and the many factors that might have contributed to them. You should expect the clinician to clearly be supportive of you (though free to disagree with you respectfully), and a welcome ally in jointly addressing your problems. He or she should be clearly focused not only on reducing symptoms and addressing associated problems but also on preventing relapses. Therapy should focus on building specific skills, such as clear thinking, effective behavior, and relationship skills, and it should provide a comfortable environment for talking about and learning those skills.

You can expect an informed consent—a discussion of the therapy approaches to be used and why. You can and should be a co-designer of the treatment plan, agreeing on the goals and methods used to reach them. You can expect your opinions to be valued. You should expect your therapist to give you things to do ("homework assignments") and things to read in-between sessions and you should do them! You should expect that this person may make use of other resources (such as community support groups) that may be helpful. You should expect that everything that is said between you and your therapist be held in the strictest confidence. (Confidentiality can only be broken if you are a danger to yourself or to others, or if you are abusing a child or an elderly person.) You should *not* expect the clinician to be your friend or surrogate parent. The relationship between the two of you may become a close one, but it is still a professional one. And while you should expect a clinician to be supportive of you, you should not expect him or her to support you in every way or agree with everything you say. Consequently, you should expect to sometimes hear things you'd rather not and to be gently pushed to do things that you're a little uncomfortable with since going beyond your "comfort zone," is where growth occurs. You should expect prompt return phone calls, but you should not expect to have spontaneous sessions over the phone except in the most urgent of circumstances. You should expect to discuss openly any and all factors affecting your work together, including time, money, schedules, expectations, disappointments, rate of progress, and the quality of your relationship. In short, you should expect professionalism provided in the service of clear therapeutic goals.

#48 Talk Therapies Can Work, But Some Talk *Therapists* Work Better Than Others

With all that we have learned about the complexity of depression, especially the fact that it is not a singular disorder with one cause and one treatment, it is apparent that treatment needs to be as multi-dimensional as the disorder. To focus on only the physiology of depression with medications or brain treatments misses the other social and psychological factors that also contribute to depression. Likewise, to just explore and express your feelings, or to just learn to recognize cognitive distortions (errors in thinking) misses too many other factors that are worthy of consideration because of their impact.

The mental health profession has been challenged over recent years to demonstrate empirically (scientifically) that the therapies they promote as effective really *are* effective. Research studies attempt to find empirical support—or lack of—for different treatments in order to compile lists of treatments that can be deemed "empirically valid" or "empirically supported" therapies.

It's important to be an informed consumer and learn something about the merits of the treatment a psychotherapist intends to provide you. But it's also important to appreciate that the therapy isn't what resolves your depression. Rather, it's the quality of the relationship you have with the therapist and the way the therapist provides the therapy, using not only good techniques but also sound judgment in applying those techniques. Good clinical judgment is essential and it's what you'll need to learn about your therapist as you begin working with him or her.

On the science side of the equation, there have been many different approaches to psychotherapy developed over the years. An approach called cognitive-behavioral therapy (CBT) has been subjected to the most research and has been shown to be an effective approach for treating depression for most people. Other approaches found to be helpful in treating depression are called interpersonal therapy (IPT) and behavioral activation (BA) therapy. Each of these therapeutic approaches involves teaching skills: CBT in thinking and information processing, IPT in relationships and social skills, and BA in effective behavior management.

This is the most important piece of information I can provide about seeking therapy. If you think going to a therapist means sitting around just talking about your childhood then I'm happy to be the one to tell you that is *not* what your therapy should be about in order to help manage your depression. You don't need to go for years, and you don't need to endlessly analyze your past. Rather, you need to know what *to do* to change your specific patterns of depression. Therapy for depression can be and usually is short term and effective. But, maintaining the relationship with your therapist may be an ideal way to have a "touchstone" for occasional reality checks and booster sessions. These are sessions that can help get you through some specific challenging time in your life or boost you through a vulnerable time so as to prevent a relapse into depression.

Couples therapy, family therapy, and many other approaches too numerous to mention can each offer some benefit to you depending on their focus and relevance for your needs. But there are also many treatments that people promote that not only don't work but *can't* work for depression because they don't address the core patterns of depression (e.g., internal orientation, past orientation, global thinking, etc.) or teach the relevant skills. So, the judgment of the therapist is important, but so is *your* judgment as an educated consumer. (Hopefully this book has helped you to be better informed about depression and thus a better-informed consumer of therapy services.)

The treatment should be informative, supportive, and with clear goals. You are half of the therapeutic relationship, so it will be critically important that you be an active partner in shaping the direction the therapy needs to take to be of maximum benefit to you. Decisions about whether a spouse or family members should be included in the therapy, whether or not the addition of medications may be helpful and other such decisions are to be made together jointly and with careful consideration.

A good therapist is worth his or her weight in *platinum*. It's wise to take the time it takes to find one.

#49 Clinical Hypnosis and Mindful Meditation Can Enhance the Treatment Process

I am and have been a strong advocate for the clinical use of hypnosis in treating depression throughout my career. I have written several books and many articles on the subject. Hypnosis, meditation (sometimes called mindfulness meditation), and other similar approaches that place an emphasis on focusing your attention and learning to regulate your emotional responses are incredibly valuable approaches.

It's important to appreciate that hypnosis and meditation are components of a larger therapy plan, practical *tools* to use, and effective vehicles for helping you absorb new ideas and develop new skills. But they are not generally considered therapies in their own right Instead, they are tools to be integrated into therapies for depression such as CBT, IPT and BA. They are easily integrated into such approaches, and many clinicians do this quite effectively.

It is important to understand this point because hypnosis and mindfulness are becoming more readily available and aggressively marketed to the general public to address many of the problems we all face. From stress and anxiety to pain management, these tools can be effective, but I want you to be an educated consumer.

There are many people who offer hypnosis or mindfulness meditation services that do not necessarily have training or background in therapy or specifically working with depressed clients. I strongly encourage you to start by finding someone with experience in these areas first and then ask whether they have additional training with hypnosis and mindfulness.

Mindful meditation and hypnosis teach focus, relaxation, and also emphasize a greater level of acceptance of life experiences. It's a valid recognition that often people's misery comes from being unable to accept the reality of some painful circumstance, leading them to fight against whatever is going on when there is no way to win the fight. Learning to deal with life as it is rather than how you wish it would be can be a sensible approach, and the various focusing skills themselves can teach you greater emotional control.

Depression can lead you to focus on the hurts of the unchangeable past while these techniques can be structured to focus you instead on the positive potentials of the future. Depression can lead you to focus on what's wrong while these techniques can be structured to shift your focus more to noticing what's right. The technique of noticing and focusing daily on things you're grateful for has been shown to be an effective approach to overcoming depression, and its value seems to be an enduring one.

These and similar approaches are very empowering. Countering the helplessness of depression and empowering people is vital to success.

#50 Prevention Is Better Than Treatment

One of the biggest changes that has occurred since I've been studying depression and treating depressed clients over the last three decades is that we've learned about strategies of prevention and that they work. There are things we know that can prevent a recurrence of depression if you've already experienced it or preventing it from appearing at all. No one is immune to depression. If you're capable of experiencing moods, then you're also capable of experiencing mood disorders. Many of the factors that can help insulate you against depression or prevent relapses have been identified throughout this book, but several key ones will be mentioned again here:

1. Critical thinking skills that help you evaluate the merits of information and people's opinions as well as the qualities of your own expectations and beliefs.

2. Reality-testing skills that help you go beyond your own thoughts and feelings in an effort to be more realistic about what's going on.

3. Social skills to help you build warm, supportive relationships that provide you with feedback and alternative viewpoints to consider as well as opportunities to get out of yourself (internal orientation).

4. Positive coping skills for doing things that help you manage stress without turning it against yourself by engaging in self- destructive behavior or against others by saying and doing things you can't take back.

5. Self-awareness to help you make better decisions that are consistent with your values and abilities.

Teaching these skills to young people, or people of *any* age for that matter, holds great potential to significantly reduce the odds of suffering depression. Having the skills in place before hard times hit can make all the difference in the world as to how things get handled when they do. It's also very important that when you recover from an episode of depression that you are well aware of the small signs that might indicate you're starting to slide. Learning to think preventively means that if you start to slide you take steps right away to prevent sliding very far. To reconnect with a therapist at such times is a sign of good judgment and a refusal to go backward and suffer through another episode.

When I first began studying depression all those years ago, treatment for depression was nearly non-existent. The idea of prevention thus seemed merely a fantasy. It should tell you something about how far we've come in understanding and treating depression to be able to document the merits of both treatment *and* prevention strategies.

There is and likely always will be much more for us to learn about depression, but it's becoming less mysterious all the time. *There's good reason to be optimistic.*

Final Thoughts

It is a human failing to not pay serious attention to a problem until it is in the "critical danger" zone, but you don't have to go through that type of failing. This book provides some key information about depression and equips you with many of the facts and perspectives you need to start to deal with and resolve depression realistically and effectively.

The most powerful tool is knowledge. I hope you will use what you have learned here to get the help you need for yourself or for those you love who may be suffering. Don't wait. Time is much too valuable a resource to waste.

Michael D. Yapko, PhD
Clinical Psychologist
www.yapko.com

Appendix A
Things to Do

Throughout this book I have made a point of saying how vitally important it is to be active in your efforts to overcome depression. That means doing things to help yourself acquire both the information and skills that can empower you to not only feel better, but *be* better in terms of how you approach life's many challenges.

In a number of places, I mentioned examples of exercises I strongly encourage my clients and you to do to facilitate overcoming depression. In order to make these exercises easier for you to access, I have listed them below. I have also identified the specific section in the book where the exercise is described in some detail with an explanation for its value.

This list of exercises is just a sample of things that can help, not a complete list. For a more comprehensive list of skill building exercises, please see my books, *Breaking the Patterns of Depression* and *Depression is Contagious*, as well as the other books in Appendix B.

When someone is depressed, asking him or her to do *anything* can seem overwhelming. So, there is no mandate to do all of them right away. Perhaps you can pick one exercise on the list that seems like it may be helpful to you and just do that one today. Take the time to develop your plan of what you will do *today.*

Maybe you're the type of person who likes to use a notepad or maybe you're more the type who likes to organize on your phone, tablet or computer. Whatever approach you prefer to use, just do it! Tomorrow, you can pick another one to do or if you want to do the same one again, that's fine. These exercises can help you reach the eventual goal of developing new and effective ways of thinking, feeling and behaving.

Identify your risk factors (#6)

List positive events on a daily basis (#10)

Physical exercise (#12)

Addressing sleep (#13)

List positive events from your history (#15)

Reality test (#18)

Generate multiple viewpoints (#19)

Identify your resources (#21)

Assess controllability (#22)

What is your code to live by? (#26)

Doing fun things (#30)

What's your mission? (#31)

Flow of steps (#32)

Observe/model others' skills (#35)

Take a technology break (#36)

Assess your impact on others (#37)

Be ready for manipulation (#41)

Learn to do self-hypnosis or meditation (#49)

Appendix B
Suggested Readings and Additional Resources

Books with a Practical Emphasis

Breaking the Patterns of Depression by Michael D. Yapko. New York: Random House Doubleday, 1997.

Depression is Contagious by Michael D. Yapko. New York: The Free Press, 2009.

Feeling Good: The New Mood Therapy by David Burns. New York: Harper, 2008.

Hand-Me-Down Blues by Michael D. Yapko. New York: St. Martins Press, 1999.

The How of Happiness: A New Approach to Getting the Life You Want by Sonja Lyubomirsky. New York: Penguin Books, 2008.

The Mindful Way through Depression: Freeing Yourself from Chronic Unhappiness by Mark Williams, John Teasdale, Zindel Segal and Jon Kabat-Zinn. New York: Guilford, 2007.

Mind Over Mood, Second edition: Change How You Feel by Changing the Way You Think by Dennis Greenberger and Christine Padesky. New York: Guilford, 2015.

Undoing Depression: What Therapy Doesn't Teach You and Medication Can't Give You by Richard O'Connor. New York: Little, Brown and Company, 2010.

Audio Self-Help Programs by Michael D. Yapko, PhD

Focusing on Feeling Good: A Skill-Building, Experiential Self-Management Program for Overcoming Depression

I emphasized the value of learning focusing techniques to help manage your mood. This *Focusing on Feeling Good* audio program was designed to teach you these skills and use them to focus on ideas and observations that can be helpful to you. It isn't something you read. It's something you *do*. There are eight sessions in this audio program including the initial session describing how you can use self-focusing exercises to overcome depression. The remaining seven sessions address the common symptom patterns associated with depression.

Here are the contents of this program:

1 Depression as the Problem: Hypnosis as the Solution (A discussion about how to manage depression skillfully)

2: The Power of Vision (The importance of goals in overcoming past and present hurts)

3: Try Again… But Do Something Different (The importance of developing the flexibility to learn new skills)

4: Good Night… and Sleep Well (Slowing down your mind and body to improve your sleep)

5: Is it in Your Control? (Learning to better distinguish what is and is not controllable)

6: Presumed Innocent but Feeling Guilty (Resolving feelings of guilt)

7: You're the Border Patrol (Learning to build and maintain self-protective boundaries)

8: Prevention Whenever Possible (Learning to think in terms of preventing depression)

Available for purchase on www.yapko.com as either a download or hard copy.

Calm Down: A Self-Help Program for Managing Anxiety

Anxiety and depression typically occur together in adults. Professionals refer to this as "co-morbidity." Learning to manage anxiety can be every bit as important as learning to manage your mood. To help in this endeavor, I have created an audio program called *Calm Down* that can help you develop specific skills in reducing and even preventing anxiety problems.

There are eight sessions in this audio program including the initial session describing how you can use self-focusing exercises to overcome anxiety. The remaining seven sessions address the common symptom patterns associated with anxiety.

Here are the contents of this program:

1. Anxiety: What it is, Where it Comes From, and What Can Help (A discussion about how to better understand and manage anxiety skillfully).

2. Change as a Process: From Fear to Acceptance Without Thinking Too Much (The importance of adapting to changes in life without over analyzing them).

3. Comfortable Familiarity and Seeking Out What's New (Sensible and positive ways of venturing outside your comfort zone).

4. Thinking Globally But Acting Locally (The danger of thinking in overly general terms and missing helpful opportunities).
5. Separate This From That (A divide-and-conquer strategy for rising above fear and self doubt).
6. Sleep Well (A soothing journey into a good quality sleep which has restorative benefits).
7. It Seems Risky... or Am I Just Too Cautious? (A focus on assessing risks realistically and enhancing trust in yourself).
8. Looking Forward (The importance of considering the future... but without the catastrophes).

Available for purchase on www.yapko.com as either a download or hard copy.

Sleeping Soundly: Enhancing Your Ability to Sleep Well Using Hypnosis.

There are two sessions in this audio program. The first one is informational and provides an overview of insomnia and its relationship to the way you think and problem-solve. The second session provides a conversational hypnosis session for you to listen to, experience, and learn from while developing the ability to sleep well. The session is soothing, supportive and provides an easy path to follow into a good night's sleep.

Available for purchase on www.yapko.com as either a download or hard copy.

Subject Index

About Dr. Michael Yapko

Michael D. Yapko, PhD, is a clinical psychologist residing near San Diego, California. He is the author of thirteen books and an editor for three books. These include his well-known books on depression; *Breaking the Patterns of Depression, Depression is Contagious,* and *Hand-Me-Down Blues.* He has published dozens of articles regarding the active treatment of depression and also authored the authoritative section on treating depression for the *Encyclopedia Britannica Medical Health Annual* in 1997. Dr. Yapko has been invited to present his ideas and strategic treatment methods to professional audiences all over the world, having lectured in more than thirty countries across six continents.

Dr. Yapko has been a passionate advocate for redefining how we think about and treat depression. He has been a vocal critic of medicalizing depression by calling it an illness or disease when there is substantial evidence that depression is about much more than biology alone. He further questions the common treatment approach of simply medicating people with drugs whose safety and efficacy are dubious. Instead, he points to the increase in depression sufferers around the world as greater evidence for it being more of a social problem than a medical problem. He emphasizes all we have learned from studying effective treatments, especially how important it is to empower people to evolve better skills in coping and problem solving, as well as other key life-management skills. Dr. Yapko's major point is both simple and compelling: Tough things happen in life and people who have the skills to manage their lives, including their moods, do better than those who don't. Beyond effective *treatment*, he also highlights the role of skill building in developing strategies of *prevention*.

Dr. Yapko has received many professional honors for his contributions to the advancement of psychotherapy. He maintains his dedication to making depression more understandable and more skillfully managed for professionals providing treatment as well as individuals suffering depression. More information about Dr. Yapko and additional helpful resources are available on his website, www.yapko.com.